D1583280

ALICE IN WATERLAND

ALICE IN WATERLAND

~

LEWIS CARROLL
and the
RIVER THAMES
in
OXFORD

To Cynthia ~

Mark Davies

MARK J. DAVIES

Signal Books
OXFORD
in association with Oxford Towpath Press

First published in the UK in 2010 by
Signal Books Limited
36 Minster Road
Oxford
OX4 1LY

www.signalbooks.co.uk

This cloth edition published 2012

Published in association with the Oxford Towpath Press

A catalogue record for this book is available from the British Library.

ISBN 978-1-908493-69-9 Cloth

Designed by Bryony Clark

Printed & bound in Great Britain
by TJ International Ltd, Padstow, Cornwall

CONTENTS

List of maps & illustrations		vi
Foreword		ix
Preface		xi
Some important dates		xiii
1	Godstow	3
2	Port Meadow	15
3	Binsey	21
4	Four Streams and Jericho	29
5	Folly Bridge	37
6	Alice's Shop	41
7	Trill Mill Stream	47
8	Christ Church Meadow	49
9	River Cherwell	59
10	Iffley Lock	67
11	Rose Island	73
12	Sandford-On-Thames	77
13	Nuneham	87
14	'The End of My Move'	97

APPENDICES

1:	*Prickett Families of Binsey and Thame*	100
2:	*Trill Mill Stream*	105
3:	*Hatter Matter*	107
4:	*Oxford College Barges*	117
5:	*The Oxford–Cambridge Boat Race of 1843*	119

Sources and Further Reading	122
Index	124

MAPS & ILLUSTRATIONS

MAPS

MAP 1: Godstow to Abingdon — 1

MAP 2: Godstow and Port Meadow — 2

MAP 3: Four Streams to Rose Island — 28

MAP 4: Sandford to Nuneham — 76

MAP 5: Nuneham to Clifton Hampden — 86

ILLUSTRATIONS

1. 'The Thames, near Godstow' (1878) — 3

2. Godstow (c1880) — 6

3. Father William (Tenniel) — 12

4. 'Barges at Binsey' (1886) — 15

5. King's horses and King's men (Tenniel) — 16

6. Medley (c1880) — 20

7. 'From the Thames, near Binsey-Green' (1848) — 21

8. The Binsey 'treacle well' (2010) — 26

9. Alice Liddell Door, Osney (2010) — 29

10. 'The Observatory and Printing Office', Jericho (c1851) — 34

11. Folly Bridge (early 1870s) — 38

12. The Sheep's Shop (Tenniel) — 40

13. Sketch of Alice Liddell, aged 8 (Carroll) — 43

14. 'The Inundation of Christchurch Meadows' (1852) — 44

15. 'A Punting Scene by the Christ Church Meadows' (c1850) — 49

16. Grandpont House, Folly Bridge (1900) — 54

17. College barges at Christ Church Meadow (c1870) — 59

18. Magdalen Tower and Bridge (1855) — 62

19. 'The Oxford Commemoration' (1863) — 65

20. 'Starting the Favorite', Isis Tavern (c1860) — 67

21. 'A Picnic to Nuneham: in Iffley Lock' (1882) — 70

22. Photograph of Alice Liddell, aged 8 (Carroll) — 72

23. The Swan Inn on Rose Island (1885) — 73

24. 'Sandford Mill' (1878) — 77

25. The Pool of Tears (Carroll) — 82

26. The Caucus-race (Tenniel) — 83

27. Nuneham House (mid-nineteenth century) — 87

28. 'Cottages at Nuneham Courtenay' (1859) — 94

29. Mary Prickett — 104

30. Alice and the Red Queen (Tenniel) — 104

31. Alderman Thomas Randall — 111

32. The Dormouse and the Hatter (Tenniel) — 112

33. Thomas Randall — 112

34. Randall family and friends (c1864/65) — 114

35. 'State Barges' (1859) — 118

FOREWORD

Many people are unaware that *Alice's Adventures in Wonderland* was inspired by a river trip that included the author, his friend, and three young children. Lorina, Alice, and Edith Liddell encouraged the telling of the tale, but it was Alice who asked Lewis Carroll to write down the story, thus preserving a spontaneous adventure that could so easily have been lost to memory.

This merry crew appear in the story from time to time, sometimes moderately disguised, and there are many references to Oxford – its events and personalities.

Alice in Waterland is the only book I am aware of that focuses on the rivers of Oxford that provide the background to the famous river-trip and other excursions with the Liddells. Mark Davies quotes both *Alice* books for all appropriate river references, and adds extracts from Lewis Carroll's private diaries to set the scene. Profusely illustrated with maps, photographs, and other images of the day, his book brings the locations of the story vividly to life.

The book includes much background information drawn from other contemporary writers to help us empathise with the Victorian times and events. Thorough research provides much that is not found elsewhere in Carroll biographies, and corrects a few long-standing errors about the people and places involved in the making of this most famous of children's stories.

EDWARD WAKELING
editor of *Lewis Carroll's Diaries*

ix

PREFACE

'There ought to be a book written about me, that there ought!' says Alice in *Alice's Adventures in Wonderland*. And there was, of course: first the fantasy from which Alice's statement comes, then a sequel, and countless books of analysis, reminiscence, and comment ever since.

Strangely, none of the writers of these books has ever approached this world-famous subject in a world-famous city from the crucial perspective of the River Thames. Yet the influence of the river in the creation of *Wonderland* and *Through the Looking-Glass* is enormous. Indeed, had there been no river, there would have been no 'Alice'. The river provided the opportunities to invent many of the tales, created the conditions for the decision to write them down, and inspired many of the two books' episodes.

It is the latter point which is of greatest interest to me, as a lover of local history. Lewis Carroll's supposed and actual use of real places, people, and incidents has produced many theories over the years. It has been pleasing to provide, from the perspective of the riverbank, confirmatory, additional, or new information relating to these ideas. It has also been gratifying, and a little surprising, to learn so much about Victorian Oxford through characters of fantasy such as the Hatter, the Sheep, and the Red Queen!

In terms of conventions, the day of the week has been included in the extracts from Lewis Carroll's diaries only when deemed important to the context of the comment. Biographical footnotes have not been provided for any individuals whose roles do not extend beyond being merely occasional companions of Carroll. For such individuals, and indeed to learn more about every aspect of Carroll's life, I suggest that readers consult Edward Wakeling's *Lewis Carroll's Diaries*. Charles Dodgson's penname of Lewis Carroll has been used throughout, save for in the 'Important Dates' section, where a real life deserved, I felt, a real name.

The images have been selected to try to convey the river scene as it would have appeared to Carroll and the Liddell girls from the 1850s to the 1870s. The earliest engraving is from 1848 (two years before Carroll's arrival in Oxford); the latest photograph is dated 1900 (two years after his death). The excerpts from novels and memoirs fall occasionally outside the direct experience of the protagonists, but nonetheless help to portray and explain a river where things tend in any case to change but slowly.

My thanks for assistance in producing this book go (in more or less chronological order) to Luke Gander, in whose shop the idea first occurred; my brother Nic ap Glyn for early feedback; Judith Curthoys, Christ Church archivist; Mark Richards and Edward Wakeling of the Lewis Carroll Society; Philip Pullman (also for his crucial role in the ongoing campaign to preserve a boatyard facility in Jericho); Catherine Robinson and Bryony Clark, editor and designer respectively; James Ferguson of Signal Books; Stephanie Jenkins, whose www.headington. org website has been an invaluable research tool; Tim Metcalfe at the *Oxford Times*; Karl Wallendszus for the photograph of the Liddell door; Tim Cox at Oxford Town Hall and David Pennant for the photographs of Thomas Randall; John Stainer and David Clark for the Randall and Spiers diary extracts respectively; Valerie Petts for the cover illustrations; and Adrian Arbib for photographing them.

In addition I would like to acknowledge the ever-helpful staff at Oxford's Bodleian Library and Centre for Oxfordshire Studies.

MARK JOHNSTONE DAVIES
'Bill the Lizard', Oxford Canal,
Oxford, June 2012

xii

SOME IMPORTANT DATES

27 Jan. 1832   Charles Lutwidge Dodgson (1832–1898) born. His parents,
                Rev. Charles (1800–1868) and Frances Jane (née Lutwidge)
                Dodgson (1803–1851), already had two daughters:
                Frances/'Fanny' (1828–1903) and Elizabeth (1830–1916).
                Subsequent children were:
                Caroline (1833–1904), Mary (1835–1911), Skeffington (1836–1919),
                Wilfred (1838–1914), Louise (1840–1930), Margaret (1841–1915),
                Henrietta (1843–1922), and Edwin (1846–1918).

24 Jan. 1851   Dodgson commenced studies at Christ Church. He graduated
                with a third-class degree in classics and a first in mathematics
                at the end of 1854.

4 May 1852   Alice Pleasance Liddell (1852–1934) born.
                Her relevant siblings were Edward Henry/'Harry' (1847–1911),
                Lorina Charlotte (1849–1930), Edith Mary (1854–1876),
                and Rhoda Caroline Anne (1859–1949), the only one to be
                born in Oxford.

7 June 1855   The appointment of Alice's father, Henry George Liddell
                (1811–1898), as Dean of Christ Church, as noted in
                Dodgson's diary.

25 Feb. 1856   Dodgson's first diary reference to the Liddell children.

1 March 1856   'Lewis Carroll' chosen as Charles Dodgson's pen-name.

25 April 1856   Dodgson's first introduction to Alice.

3 June 1856   First known boat trip with Harry Liddell.

5 June 1856   First known boat trip with Ina Liddell.

[Diaries for April 1858–May 1862 missing.]

22 Dec. 1861   Dodgson ordained by the Bishop of Oxford.

26 May 1862   First known boat trip with Alice Liddell.

4 July 1862   The boat trip to Godstow, acknowledged as the day the story was created. Dodgson began writing in earnest on 13 November 1862, finished on 10 February 1863, and presented the handwritten manuscript of 'Alice's Adventures under Ground' to Alice on 26 November 1864.

25 June 1863   Last boat trip with the Liddell sisters.

14 May 1865   Dodgson preached first Oxford sermon, at St Paul's, Jericho.

4 July 1865   *Alice's Adventures in Wonderland* printed, then recalled, and republished later that year.

6 Dec. 1871   First copy of *Through the Looking-Glass* received by Dodgson, although published as '1872'. Further editions were dated 1878, 1887, and 1897 (the same year that ed. 9 of *Wonderland* was published).

15 Sept. 1880   Alice Liddell married Reginald Hargreaves.

22 Dec. 1886   *Alice's Adventures under Ground*, Dodgson's handwritten original four chapters, published in facsimile.

14 Jan. 1898   Death of Charles Dodgson.

16 Nov. 1934   Death of Alice Hargreaves (née Liddell).

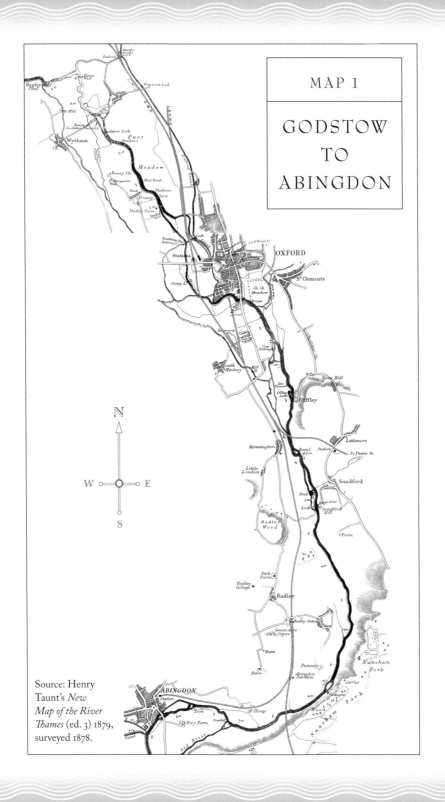

MAP 1

GODSTOW
TO
ABINGDON

Source: Henry Taunt's *New Map of the River Thames* (ed. 3) 1879, surveyed 1878.

MAP 2

GODSTOW AND PORT MEADOW

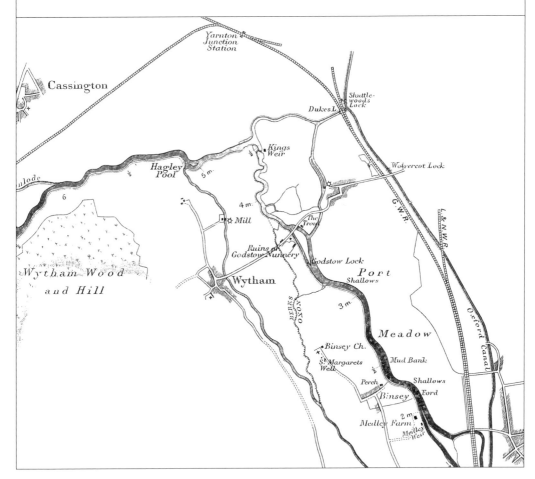

Source: Henry Taunt's *New Map of the River Thames* (ed. 3) 1879, surveyed 1878.

1

GODSTOW

1. 'The Thames, near Godstow' from Alfred Rimmer's *Pleasant Spots Around Oxford* (1878).

3

Diary

19 MAY 1857

Walked with Skeffington* to Godstow, where, oddly enough, I do not remember ever being before.

3 JULY 1862 (Thurs.)

Atkinson and I went to lunch at the Deanery, after which we were to have gone down the river with the children, but as it rained, we remained to hear some music and singing instead. The three sang 'Sally come up' with great spirit. Then croquêt, at which Duckworth joined us, and he and Atkinson afterwards dined with me. I mark this day with a white stone.†

4 JULY 1862 (Fri.)

Duckworth and I made an expedition up the river to Godstow with the three Liddells: we had tea on the bank there, and did not reach Ch. Ch. again till quarter past eight. ‡

---

* Skeffington Dodgson (1836–1919) was the brother next in age to Charles, who was the oldest boy in a family of eleven children (see page xiii).

† Carroll applied the term 'white stone day' to days of outstanding significance. The phrase was used in ancient Rome, and also occurs in the Bible (Revelations 2:17). It is noticeable that the day of the all-important river trip to Godstow in 1862 did not rate this assessment.

‡ Another later note opposite the entry for 4 July 1862 reveals Carroll's subsequent deliberations over the title of his story: 'Alice's Adventures Underground' (10 February 1863); 'Alice's Hour in Elfland' (9 June 1864); 'Alice's Adventures in Wonderland' (28 June 1864). He settled on the former in the handwritten manuscript that he presented to Alice on 26 November 1864, a date also noted in this sequence. It was an expanded version of this original offering that was published as *Alice's Adventures in Wonderland*, and the importance of the 4th of July is further emphasised by the date selected for publication: 4 July 1865. 'Under Ground' was published separately in facsimile in 1886.

ON THE OPPOSITE PAGE, IN A NOTE DATED 10 FEB. 1863:

On which occasion I told them the fairy-tale of "Alice's Adventures Under Ground", which I undertook to write out for Alice, and which is now finished (as to the text) though the pictures are not yet nearly done.

3 AUG. 1862 (Sun.)

Went over to the Deanery to ask if they could come with us to Nuneham on Wednesday, as Harcourt* was writing to his relations at Nuneham House, and found the children at dinner, at which I joined them.

6 AUG. 1862 (Wed.)

In the afternoon Harcourt and I took the three Liddells up to Godstow, where we had tea: we tried the game of "the Ural Mountains" on the way, but it did not prove very successful, and I had to go on with my interminable fairy-tale of "Alice's Adventures". We got back soon after 8.

A very enjoyable expedition, the last, I should think, to which Ina is likely to be allowed to come.

NOTE ON PAGE OPPOSITE:

Her 14th time.[†]

---

* Augustus George Vernon Harcourt (1834–1919) was the cousin of Edward William Harcourt (1825–1891), the heir to Nuneham House, a popular destination for boating parties on the Thames several miles downstream (see page 91).

† The first river outing with Alice's older sister Lorina, always known as Ina, had taken place on 5 June 1856, when she had just turned seven. Alice's first known river trip was on 26 May 1862 (see page 68), though she had certainly been on other excursions before this.

2. Godstow (c1880), looking north, and showing The Trout public house and the bridge which takes the road to Wytham over the Thames. *(Images & Voices, Oxfordshire County Council)*

GODSTOW

It was on the bank of the Thames near the hamlet of Godstow, some three miles north of Oxford, that the phenomenon of 'Alice' had its birth. Here it was, on Friday 4 July 1862, that the Oxford don Charles Lutwidge Dodgson, later to achieve worldwide fame as Lewis Carroll, and his friend Robinson Duckworth stopped for a picnic with three young sisters called Liddell. They had rowed upstream that day from the Oxford college of Christ Church, where Carroll (then aged 30) lived and worked and where the girls – Lorina (aged 13), Alice (10), and Edith (8) – resided as daughters of the Dean, Henry Liddell.* There was nothing especially unusual about this particular fivesome going out on the river together; nor was it out of the ordinary for Carroll to invent stories that day to keep the girls amused. But the date is enshrined in the history of children's literature as the one when Alice persuaded the versatile mathematics don to write down these impromptu stories for her.

Carroll's immediate diary comment on the day was brief and unremarkable: 'Duckworth and I made an expedition up the river to Godstow with the three Liddells: we had tea on the bank there.' It is Carroll's later addition which defines the day's supreme significance: 'On which occasion I told them the fairy-tale of "Alice's Adventures Underground", which I undertook to write out for Alice.' To emphasise the point, the subtitle he subsequently selected was 'A Christmas Gift to a Dear Child in Memory of a Summer Day'.

---

* Henry George Liddell (1811–98) was a former graduate of Christ Church. He married Lorina Reeve (1826–1910) in 1846, and moved into the Deanery at Christ Church in 1855, joined early the following year by his wife and family.

Published accounts of the day by any of the participants are rare. Carroll himself made only one, writing in *The Theatre* of April 1887 (as reproduced in the *Lewis Carroll Picture Book*, edited by Carroll's nephew, Stuart Dodgson Collingwood, in 1899):

Many a day had we rowed together on that quiet stream – the three little maidens and I – and many a fairy tale had been extemporised for their benefit … yet none of these many tales got written down: they lived and died, like summer midges, each in its own golden afternoon until there came a day when, as it chanced, one of my listeners petitioned that the tale might be written out for her.

In the same publication, Collingwood reprinted a letter from Canon Duckworth,* written about 1897, giving his recollection of 'the famous Long Vacation voyage to Godstow' with Carroll. There he wrote that 'I rowed *stroke* and he rowed *bow* … and the story was actually composed and spoken over my *shoulder* for the benefit of Alice Liddell, who was acting as "cox" of our gig'.

Alice herself ventured only two printed recollections: a very brief one in the third chapter of Collingwood's *Life and Letters of Lewis Carroll* (1898), and more informatively via her son, Caryl Hargreaves (1887–1955), in the *Cornhill Magazine* of July 1932, when Alice was 80 years old. In the latter, she emphasised the privileged nature of the role referred to by Duckworth, that of the cox: 'Sometimes (a treat of great importance in the eyes of the fortunate one) one of us was allowed to take the tiller ropes: and, if the course was a little devious, little blame was accorded to the small but inexperienced coxswain.'

---

* Robinson Duckworth (1834–1911) was a fellow of Trinity College from 1860 to 1876, and a Canon of Westminster from 1875.

In the same *Cornhill* article, Alice affirmed that Duckworth was most often the other adult on these rowing trips, saying: 'We went on the river for the afternoon with Mr Dodgson ... at most four or five times every summer term.' Most of these trips took them downstream from Christ Church. The journey of 4 July 1862 was unusual in that they went up the river. Of the many boating trips which Carroll noted between the first in June 1856 and last in June 1863, only two took them to Godstow,* or indeed anywhere upstream of Christ Church, and it is significant that in his diary entry for the day Carroll stressed the word 'up' the river, to indicate its unusual nature.

The only other known trip to Godstow came a month later, on 6 August 1862, when Augustus Harcourt, another Christ Church academic, was the other adult. On this occasion, Carroll noted his attempt to amuse the girls with a game, but then had to accede to their requests 'to go on with my interminable fairy-tale', which he was already referring to as 'Alice's Adventures'. It may be significant that these two Godstow trips are the only ones when any specific reference is made by Carroll to story-telling. A possible conclusion is that this route – initially past the working-class suburb of St Ebbe's, the city gas-works, and the developing suburb of Osney Town – presented fewer diversions for the children. Downstream from Christ Church the banks of the Thames were (and still are to this day) almost instantly rural in nature, there were places to stop for refreshments, and the river would have presented scenes of a generally busier and more entertaining nature.

So it may well have been the comparatively unremarkable nature of the Thames upstream of Christ Church which was the main factor in the creation of 'Alice' on Friday 4 July 1862 – in which

---

* Carroll's first ever visit to Godstow, and its atmospheric ruined nunnery, had been in May 1857.

case it was a very near thing altogether. Carroll's original intention had been to go *down* the river the day before. Had it not rained that particular Thursday, that is what they would have done, along a familiar and seemingly more stimulating route, with fewer opportunities for story-telling. Godstow had not been the first choice for the outing in August either; again Nuneham had been the preferred initial destination.

The weather on 4 July 1862 has been much debated, since the participants' memories are at odds with the Meteorological Office's record of the day as 'cool and rather wet'.* Carroll wrote in *The Theatre* (April 1887):

> Full many a year has slipped away, since that 'golden afternoon' that gave thee birth, but I can call it up almost as clearly as if it were yesterday – the cloudless blue above, the watery mirror below, the boat drifting idly on its way, the tinkle of the drops that fell from the oars, as they waved so sleepily to and fro, and (the one bright gleam of life in all the slumberous scene) the three eager faces, hungry for news of fairy-land, and who would not be said 'nay' to: from whose lips 'Tell us a story, please,' had all the stern immutability of Fate!

Alice's memory of the day was similar: 'Nearly all of *Alice's Adventures Underground* was told on that blazing summer afternoon with the heat haze shimmering over the meadows where the party landed to shelter for a while in the shadow cast by the haycocks near Godstow' (*Cornhill*). In the same article she observed: 'Many of my earlier adventures must be irretrievably lost to posterity, because Mr. Dodgson told us many, many stories before the famous trip on the

---

* Records taken by the Radcliffe Observatory in Oxford were 'rain after 2pm, cloud cover 10/10, and maximum shade temperature of 67.9 degrees' (Gardner, 2000).

river to Godstow.' In *Life and Letters*, Collingwood quotes Alice as saying, 'Most of Mr Dodgson's stories were told to us on river expeditions to Nuneham and Godstow' and

> I believe the beginning of 'Alice' was told one summer afternoon when the sun was so burning that we had landed in the meadows down* the river, deserting the boat to take refuge in the only shade to be found, which was under a new-made hayrick. Here from all three came the old petition of 'Tell us a story,' and so began the ever-delightful tale.

And so, from the riverside reality of that July day came the opening line of prose from *Alice's Adventures in Wonderland* – 'Alice was beginning to get very tired of sitting by her sister on the bank, and of having nothing to do' – followed immediately by Alice's headlong pursuit of the White Rabbit into his burrow. Of this crucial beginning, Carroll wrote (*The Theatre*): 'I distinctly remember ... I had sent my heroine down a rabbit-hole, to begin with, without the least idea what was to happen afterwards.' What did happen afterwards, of course, is that the story became among the most famous ever told ...

---

* Alice's use of 'down' the river, when Godstow is 'up', must have been habitual (being the direction in which they were all much more accustomed to go) rather than a faulty or conflicting memory.

3. Image from *Wonderland* by John Tenniel of 'Father William' balancing an eel in the chapter called 'Advice from a Caterpillar'. In the background are three 'bucks' (wicker eel traps), once a common sight at weirs in the Oxford area.

TEXTS

The essential role played by the Thames in the creation of 'Alice' is apparent in the poems in *Alice's Adventures in Wonderland*. The 'three' referred to are Lorina, Alice, and Edith, hence the presumed play on words between 'little' and 'Liddell':

> All in the golden afternoon
> Full leisurely we glide;
> For both our oars, with little skill
> By little arms are plied,
> While little hands make vain pretence
> Our wanderings to guide.
>
> Ah, cruel Three! In such an hour,
> Beneath such dreamy weather,
> To beg a tale of breath too weak
> To stir the tiniest feather!
> Yet what can one poor voice avail
> Against three tongues together?

The penultimate verse reads:

> Thus grew the tale of Wonderland:
> Thus slowly, one by one,
> Its quaint events were hammered out –
> And now the tale is done,
> And home we steer, a merry crew,
> Beneath the setting sun.

In *Through the Looking-Glass* (1872) there are two poems, both demonstrating that, despite a gap of many years, the river trips were still foremost in Carroll's mind. The introductory poem includes the lines:

A tale begun in other days,
When summer suns were glowing –
A simple chime, that served to time
The rhythm of our rowing.

The acrostic poem (spelling 'Alice Pleasance Liddell') at the end of *Looking-Glass* begins:

A boat beneath a sunny sky
Lingering onward dreamily
In an evening of July –

Children three that nestle near,
Eager eye and willing ear,
Pleased a simple tale to hear.

The final verse reads:

Ever drifting down the stream –
Lingering in the golden gleam –
Life, what is it but a dream?

2

PORT MEADOW

4. 'Barges at Binsey' from Alfred J. Church's *Isis and Thamesis* (1886). The scene shown is actually Medley, not Binsey, where the Thames splits into two main channels at the southern end of Port Meadow. The stream shown flows through the city as the Castle Mill Stream, of which the Trill Mill Stream (see page 47) is an offshoot. A footbridge across the other (principal) branch of the Thames here, providing pedestrian access to Binsey on the western bank, was opened in 1865. The houseboats, among Oxford's first, belonged to the rival families of boatbuilders called Beesley (far bank) and Bossom.

Diary

24 JUNE 1863 (Wed.)

Great Volunteer Review in Port Meadow. I went there with Dukes (who had to leave before it was over) and there I fell in with the Liddells, and with Hoole. We waited to see them safe off, and walked back, and dined in my rooms.

5. Image from *Looking-Glass* by John Tenniel of the King's horses and the King's men in the chapter called 'The Lion and the Unicorn'.

PORT MEADOW

Between Godstow and Oxford lies Port Meadow, some 350 acres of river floodplain, bordered by the Thames on the west and the railway to the east. Its appearance, save a southern section which has been artificially elevated through use as a rubbish dump, is much as it would have looked to the party which rowed up the river here in July 1862. The meadow has been a place of resort for Oxonians for centuries, hosting many social and sporting events, of which horse-races were of especial note, from the seventeenth century onwards.

One of *the* Oxford events of 1863 was held on Port Meadow. This was the Great Volunteer Review, a 'sham fight' involving 8,000 men from 'some of the finest bodies of cavalry, artillery, and infantry in the country', as Oxford's weekly newspaper *Jackson's Oxford Journal* described it. An estimated 40,000 to 50,000 people watched the spectacle on 24 June. Carroll was among them, likewise the Liddell family, perhaps in the grandstand erected specially for the occasion. If so, they may have been disappointed; evidently it did not provide the expected advantages. *Jackson's* commented: 'It is hardly to be wondered at that the occupants of this stand should express themselves in terms of great dissatisfaction, in witnessing less of the movements than many persons who had paid nothing.' The article continued: 'Another stand, erected on another part of the ground by Mr C. Bossom,*

---

* The Bossom family's association with the river in Oxford goes back centuries. In the second half of the nineteenth century, they and a rival family called Beesley operated boat-hire and repair facilities at Medley, where the Thames splits into two main channels at the southern edge of Port Meadow. The current boat-building firm at Medley still (2012) trades under the Bossom name. A more complete history of the colourful Bossom and Beesley families, of Oxford and Medley, appears in *A Towpath Walk in Oxford* (see page 129).

found a good number of patrons; barges were moored in the river, on which further accommodation was provided ... The manoeuvres were brought to a close at about six o'clock.'*

However much or little they saw, the excitement of the event seems likely to have been fresh in everyone's mind the next day, when Carroll escorted the whole Liddell family on a momentous river trip to Nuneham (see page 93). There is every reason to think that the battle scenes in *Looking-Glass* are a direct result. So too the White King's question to Alice in the chapter called 'The Lion and the Unicorn': 'Did you happen to see any soldiers, my dear, as you came through the wood?' 'Yes, several thousand, I should think.'

Alice was familiar with Port Meadow from a recreational perspective too, recalling that a 'great joy was to go out riding with my father ... on Port Meadow, or go to Abingdon through Radley, and there were the most lovely rides through Wytham Woods' (*Cornhill Magazine*). On the other hand, exercises of this kind also took place within the grounds of Nuneham Park itself at this time, scenes which could quite possibly have been witnessed by Carroll, given his and the Liddells' familiarity with the location and the Harcourt family (see page 93).

_____

* In *Looking-Glass*, Tweedledum and Tweedledee 'fight till six, and then have dinner'.

TEXT

Port Meadow is a vast area, noted for its distinct *lack* of trees. That apart, could this extract, from 'The Lion and the Unicorn' in *Looking-Glass*, have been inspired by the Great Volunteer Review? Having just left Humpty Dumpty, and heard a 'heavy crash', Alice watches the King's men and the King's horses pass. First the soldiers

> came running through the wood, at first in twos and threes, then ten or twenty together, and at last in such crowds that they seemed to fill the whole forest. Alice ... thought that in all her life she had never seen soldiers so uncertain on their feet: they were always tripping over something or other, and whenever one went down, several more always fell over him, so that the ground was soon covered with little heaps of men. Then came the horses. Having four feet, these managed rather better than the foot-soldiers; but even *they* stumbled now and then; and it seemed to be a regular rule that, whenever a horse stumbled, the rider fell off instantly.

6. Medley, looking north. Henry Taunt's photograph of about 1880 (see page 15 for an almost contemporary view) shows the rival boat-hire firms of Bossom (left) and Beesley (right), with the wide expanse of Port Meadow in the distance. (*Images & Voices, Oxfordshire County Council*)

7. (OPPOSITE) 'From the Thames, near Binsey-Green', first published (Charles Knight, London) in *The Land We Live In*, March 1848. The view was especially chosen because it had 'seldom, if ever, before been engraved'. In the middle ground is Port Meadow, on the far side of the river, which is crossed here apparently by a ford.

3

BINSEY

Diary

9 MAY 1875 (Sun.)

Re-opening of Binsey Church, which prevented Prout meeting me on the hill as usual. *

4 JUNE 1881 (Sat.)

As Prout was sent for yesterday to his brother in London (who died) Salwey undertook to take the service at Binsey for him, and I volunteered to help him, and prepared a short sermon. But I am not destined to deliver it, as Prout returned this evening. It is some relief to one's nerves, as I was looking forwards with terror to the ordeal. It is years since I have tried preaching. †

---

* Thomas Jones Prout (1823–1909) was a life-long friend of Carroll, who entered Christ Church in 1842, and like Carroll remained in residence there for the rest of his life.
† Although ordained as an Anglican clergyman in 1861, Carroll officiated at church services very rarely, hence his feeling of 'terror'.

BINSEY

Binsey is a hamlet of a dozen or so houses on the opposite (western) side of the Thames to Port Meadow. It forms part of the estate of Carroll's college of Christ Church, which appointed curates to the church there. Carroll's diary references to Binsey come as a result of his life-long friendship with Thomas Jones Prout, who held the living of the village's church of St Margaret from 1857 until 1891.

It was Prout who restored a well in the graveyard which had been revered for centuries as the site of the spring miraculously summoned by Oxford's patron saint, Frideswide, early in the eighth century. The reputed healing properties of the well's waters attracted huge numbers of pilgrims, and it is this well to which the Dormouse* refers at the 'Mad Tea-Party' in *Wonderland*. The three sisters at the bottom of the treacle well clearly represent the three Liddells: 'Elsie', or L. C., is Lorina Charlotte; 'Lacie' is an anagram of Alice; and 'Tillie' is short for Matilda, the pet-name given to Edith. The notion of a treacle well seems at first preposterous, yet is based on an early meaning of the word as a healing liquid or medicine (from the Greek *Thēriakē* meaning 'antidote'). So there was indeed a treacle well at Binsey, and the fictional Alice – who at first declared: 'There is no such thing!' – was wise eventually to admit that 'I dare say there may be *one*'. It is at the Party that the date of Alice's adventures is

---

* In the narrative to Carroll's *Diaries*, Edward Wakeling suggests that Prout had a 'reputation for sleeping during the long and sometimes tedious meetings held by the dons'. Given his Binsey responsibilities, he is therefore an especially good candidate for the original of the Dormouse.

revealed as 4 May – Alice Liddell's actual birthday. She is intended to be seven in the book, and is seven-and-a-half (as she tells Humpty Dumpty) in *Looking-Glass*, whose action takes place on 4 November.

In *The Book of the Thames* (1859), Mr and Mrs S. C. (Samuel Carter and Anna Maria) Hall recorded their journey from source to sea. This was the scene at Binsey, at exactly the time when Thomas Prout first assumed responsibility as curate:

> Its church has a heart-broken look; and of the well there is but an indication – a large earth-mound in a corner of the graveyard completely dried up, there being no sign of water; the spring is lost; and so, indeed, is its memory – for we inquired in vain among the neighbouring peasantry for St Margaret's Well, of which they had heard and knew nothing – *sic transit*!

Prout restored St Margaret's Well in 1874, perhaps in response to the new interest which the publication of *Looking-Glass* in 1872 must have generated. The friendship between Carroll and Prout is probably sufficient to explain why Carroll decided to include his veiled allusion to the Binsey 'treacle well'. Many Carroll commentators have suggested another reason: that Mary Prickett (1832–1920), Alice's governess, was from the village, and was therefore the source for the story. Prickett is a fairly unusual name, after all, and it has occurred in Binsey since at least the sixteenth century. Mary Prickett, however, is not from this line of the family – despite several other apparent indicators.

Mary Prickett is widely acknowledged as being the model for the Red Queen in *Looking-Glass*, a character with whom some possible Binsey associations can be discerned. Carroll never revealed the real-life inspiration for his characters, but he came very close in *The Theatre* of April 1887 when describing the Red Queen as 'a Fury, ... cold and calm; ... formal and strict, yet not unkindly; pedantic to the tenth degree, the concentrated essence of all governesses!'. In the chapter called 'The Garden of Live Flowers', the Rose calls the Red Queen 'one of the thorny kind'.* This, surely, was an allusion to the children's nickname for their governess of 'Pricks' (*Cornhill Magazine*), but additionally, given Carroll's love of wordplay, there was every reason to think† that he was combining a pun on 'Thornbury', the ancient name for the site of St Margaret's Well, with the undeniably long association of the Prickett family with the locality.

The explanation for the Red Queen's rapid increase in size is interesting too. She is three inches high initially, but grows taller than Alice when in the Garden. 'It's the fresh air that does it,' says the Rose, and 'wonderfully fine air it is, out here'. It seems just the kind of thing a local of Binsey might say, given the notoriety of Oxford's own dank and enervating climate.‡

Yet, despite these apparent clues, Mary Prickett was not descended from the Binsey Pricketts at all. Her father, James, was born in Oxford, but *his* father, and all the identifiable generations preceding, had come from the Oxfordshire town of Thame. It is certainly not impossible that there was some blood connection, and Mary actually *was* related to the Binsey Pricketts, or assumed that she was, or Carroll did. Yet the evidence of any such family relationship remains unproven (see Appendix 1). Whatever, it is certainly not true, as many texts claim, that Mary Prickett or her father came from the village.

A relatively recent successor to the Rev. Thomas Prout wrote to *Country Life* (11 April 1963) to refute a suggestion that the churchyard at Binsey was haunted. The Rev. Arnold Mallinson emphasised instead

---

* This is the phrase used in the first edition. In the second edition of 1878 it was changed to 'one of the kind that has nine spikes'.
† As I did myself, when exposing this presumed additional clue in *A Towpath Walk in Oxford* (see page 129).
‡ In 1895 Alphonse Daudet (1840–97) summed up the opinions of successive earlier writers with his succinct assessment of Christ Church Meadow as '*le rheumatisme vert*' (Jan Morris, *Oxford Book of Oxford*, 1978).

'the powerful holiness of the place occasioned by the existence of the well of St Margaret at the west end of the church'. In the same letter he added that 'when the Rev. Mr Prout restored the well in the 19th century he asked Lewis Carroll about it'. Carroll's response of 'Leave WELL alone!' is a joke he employed in his text, the Dormouse telling Alice that the sisters were not merely in the well, but 'well in' it!

8. The 'treacle well' of St Margaret in the churchyard a little north of Binsey village. *(Mark Davies, 2010)*

TEXT

With help from the Cheshire Cat, Alice finds her way to the March Hare's House, and joins the 'Mad Tea-Party'. When Alice declines to tell a story, the Hare and the Hatter wake up the Dormouse, who begins to tell them about three little sisters who live at the bottom of a well. Alice regularly interrupts the Dormouse with questions, exactly as one might imagine her doing when Carroll was first inventing the story, inspired quite possibly by glimpses of Binsey church across the fields as they rowed past.

> 'What did they live on?' said Alice, who always took a great interest in questions of eating and drinking.
> 'They lived on treacle,' said the Dormouse, after thinking a minute or two...

Alice then asks, for the second time:

> 'Why did they live at the bottom of a well?'
> The Dormouse again took a minute or two to think about it, and then said, 'It was a treacle-well.'

Although the context is bizarre, the logic is undeniable! Alice promises not to interrupt, and the Dormouse continues:

> 'These three little sisters – they were learning to draw, you know –'
> 'What did they draw?' said Alice, quite forgetting her promise.
> 'Treacle,' said the Dormouse, without considering at all, this time.

Alice queries where the treacle is drawn from.

> 'You can draw water out of a water-well,' said the Hatter, 'so I should think you could draw treacle out of a treacle-well – eh, stupid.'
> 'But they were *in* the well,' Alice said to the Dormouse, not choosing to notice this last remark.
> 'Of course they were,' said the Dormouse, – 'well in.'

MAP 3

FOUR STREAMS TO ROSE ISLAND

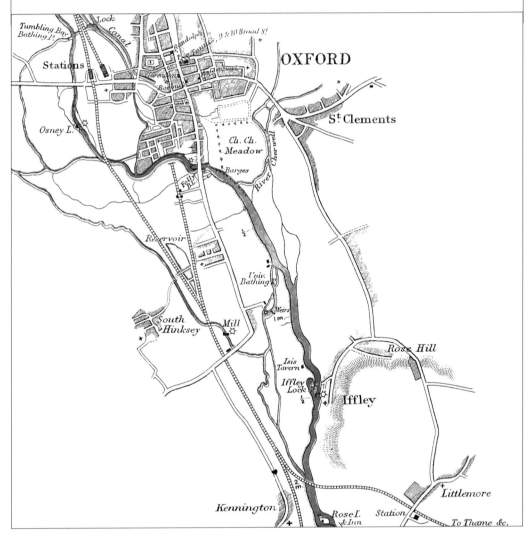

Source: Henry Taunt's *New Map of the River Thames* (ed. 3) 1879, surveyed 1878.

4

FOUR STREAMS AND JERICHO

9. Detail of door carved by Alice Liddell showing St Frideswide's arrival at Binsey by boat, prior to the events which led to the miracle of the 'treacle well'. Alice was taught art by John Ruskin (see page 35), the most influential supporter of the Pre-Raphaelite movement, which flourished in Jericho, thanks to the patronage of Thomas Combe (see page 33). The door was originally in a London church which opened in 1890, and is now displayed in St Frideswide's Church, Osney.
(Karl Wallendszus, 2010)

Diary

6 MARCH 1857

Called at the Printing Press and left a note asking Mr. Combe* if he could tell me where to get a small hand printing machine.

19 JUNE 1862

To the University Press where we† visited the pictures at Mr. Combe's.

24 FEB. 1863

In the afternoon I joined the Liddells in their walk (Alice, Edith and the governess) and went with them to leave a note at the Press (where I took them to see the printing etc. and to call on Mrs. Combe, who showed us their pictures), then to the Museum.

8 MARCH 1863 (Sun.)

Took afternoon service at Osney Chapel for Chamberlain.

I was annoyed at finding that I hesitated a good deal in the first lesson, but I got on better afterwards.

---

* Thomas Combe (1796–1872), Superintendent of Oxford University Press and a great patron of the arts (see page 33).
† Carroll had three visitors at this time, his aunt Lucy Lutwidge (1805–80), and his two older sisters Frances ('Fanny') Dodgson (1828–1903) and Elizabeth Dodgson (1830–1916). Two days earlier, Carroll's sisters had been soaked on the river, inspiring the composition of 'The Pool of Tears' (see page 80).

16 JULY 1863

Called on Mr. Combe with my first drawing on wood. Mr. Woolner* was there, just beginning a bust of Mr. Combe. He looked at the drawing (a half length of the heroine) and condemned the arms, which he says I <u>must</u> draw from the life.

19 OCT. 1863

Went to Combe's in the evening to meet the publisher Macmillan and get him to print me some of Blake's 'Songs of Innocence etc.' on large paper.

16 JUNE 1864

Took Holman Hunt.† Dined at Mr. Combe's to meet him.

14 MAY 1865 (Sun.)

Preached for Hackman‡ at St. Paul's, my first sermon in Oxford, to the largest congregation I have yet addressed, 300 or 400 I should think.

Lunched with Mr. Combe, and met Holman Hunt, Mr. & Mrs. Woolner etc.

2 AUG. 1865

Finally decided on the re-print of 'Alice', and that the first 2000 shall be sold as waste paper. Wrote about it to Macmillan, Combe, and Tenniel.

12 JULY 1876

Edwin went off to the early service at St Barnabas.§

---

* Thomas Woolner (1825–1892), the sole Pre-Raphaelite sculptor. Carroll met him again at the Combes' on 17 and 23 July. Woolner's bust of Combe is at the Ashmolean Museum.

† William Holman Hunt (1827–1910), a founder member of the Pre-Raphaelite Brotherhood.

‡ Alfred Hackman (1811–74), Christ Church chaplain 1837–73 and vicar of St Paul's 1844–71. Hackman (through Combe, assuredly) had first introduced Carroll to Hunt, on 13 June 1857.

§ Edwin Dodgson (1846–1918) was Carroll's youngest brother. This is the sole mention of Jericho's St Barnabas' Church in the diaries.

FOUR STREAMS AND JERICHO

Four Streams marks the point at which two sidestreams of the River Thames, the Bulstake Stream and Sheepwash Channel, flow away from the main north–south course of the river below Port Meadow. Until the end of the eighteenth century, when Osney Lock was fully opened, these streams constituted part of the main Thames navigation, a meandering route which obliged boats to take a troublesome westerly detour.

The Bulstake Stream remained navigable until 1853, when an open-air bathing place called Tumbling Bay (marked on the map on page 28) was established, but the Sheepwash Channel remains to this day the means by which boats move between the Thames and Isis Lock (formerly known as 'Louse Lock'), the junction with the Oxford Canal. A little north of the lock, adjacent to the canal, is the suburb of Jericho. Part of what the poet Gerard Manley Hopkins called in 1866 Oxford's 'base and brickish skirt',* Jericho was constructed initially to provide accommodation for workers at the newly relocated Oxford University Press, which began printing there in 1830. The managing partner of the Bible side of the Press from

---

* *Duns Scotus's Oxford*. By contrast, in the same poem Hopkins describes collegiate Oxford as:

  Towery city, and branchy between towers;
  Cuckoo-echoing, bell-swarmed, lark-charmed, rook-racked, river-rounded.

  Gerard Manley Hopkins (1844–89) also wrote *Binsey Poplars felled 1879*, a lament for some distinctive riverside trees to the north of the village which were cut down for railway use. Hopkins loved Oxford's rivers, and described exploring them by canoe as 'paradisiacal' and 'the summit of human happiness' (*A Very Private Life*, Robert Bernard Martin, 1991).

1851 until his death was Thomas Combe (1796–1872). Combe has only a passing association with either the river or the canal in Oxford, but his role in enabling the handwritten manuscript presented to one small girl to develop into the phenomenon of 'Alice' is, I hope, significant enough to warrant a slight detour from the main course of the river.

Thomas Combe lived with his wife Martha in a large house overlooking the quadrangle of the University Press, which lies in the south-eastern corner of Jericho, closest to the city. Carroll had known the couple since at least early 1857. On 19 October 1863, Combe introduced Carroll to Alexander Macmillan (1813–96), who subsequently agreed to publish a revised and enlarged version of the handwritten 'Alice's Adventures under Ground' in book form. In *The Alice Companion* (1998) it is stated that 'Carroll photographed Combe who then helped him devise the trial layouts for Alice. Carroll's professionalism in page layout owed much to Combe's tuition.' In June 1865, the first 2,000 copies of *Alice's Adventures in Wonderland* were printed at the Press, and although this first print-run was recalled as substandard, mainly at the insistence of the illustrator, John Tenniel (1820–1914), the book's potential was established, and it was reprinted elsewhere for release the following year. Macmillan went on to publish all the subsequent 'Alice' titles but did not again call on the University Press to print them.

Despite this probable embarrassment for Combe, he and Carroll remained on good terms even though their religious views differed. Combe sympathised with the aspirations of the Tractarians of the 'Oxford Movement', which sought to restore elements of Catholic teaching and ritual within the Church of England. It was a cause also dear to Carroll's father, the Rev. Charles Dodgson (1800–1868), but not to Carroll himself. Yet the first sermon that Carroll ever preached

in Oxford, in May 1865, was at St Paul's, opposite the University Press, where Combe was a churchwarden. Soon after, Combe provided the funds for the new and larger High Anglican church of St Barnabas, built specifically to cater for Jericho's rapidly increasing population.*

Carroll often took visitors to view the Combes' art collection at the Press. The couple were great patrons of the arts, and are especially important for championing the works of the Pre-Raphaelite Brotherhood at a time when these artists' devotion to naturalistic detail often attracted hostility or ridicule. It was through the Combes that Carroll met artists such as John Millais, William Holman Hunt, and Dante Gabriel Rossetti. The first two men often stayed at the Combes' home, producing or completing many of their paintings there. Through this connection, Carroll, a highly accomplished early photographer, was subsequently able to take pictures of these famous men and their families, in Oxford and in London.

Another key promoter of the Pre-Raphaelites was John Ruskin (1819–1900), who graduated from Christ Church in 1843 and returned to Oxford in 1870 as the Slade Professor of Fine Art. Like Carroll, Ruskin knew the Liddell sisters personally, giving them lessons in drawing and painting. In his autobiography *Praeterita* (1885–89), Ruskin recounted the story, undated, of how he found an opportunity to see the girls one evening without their parents' knowledge, after

---

* Carroll preached rarely, but one notable example was the service that he took at Osney Chapel in March 1863, when he stood in for another Christ Church man, the Rev. Thomas Chamberlain, curate of St Thomas' parish (in which Jericho lay) from 1842 to 1892, and a high-profile supporter of Tractarianism.

10. (OPPOSITE) 'The Observatory and Printing Office' by Carl Rundt (1802–1868) from *A Walk Round Oxford* (c1851). This idealised view of the expanding suburb of Jericho shows (right) the Oxford University Press, where Thomas and Martha Combe resided, and (left) the Radcliffe Observatory (1794). The coalboat on the eighteenth-century Oxford Canal in the foreground is pointing south, towards the junction with the Thames and the canal's Oxford terminus.

complaining 'of never getting a sight of them lately, after knowing them from the nursery'. Dean and Mrs Liddell had been invited to dine at Blenheim Palace, home of the Duke of Marlborough. 'Alice said that she thought, perhaps, if I would come round after papa and mamma were safe off to Blenheim, Edith and she might give me a cup of tea and a little singing, and Rhoda show me how she was getting on with her drawing and geometry, or the like.'*

Unfortunately for Ruskin, the snow that winter's night was so bad that the Dean and his wife had to return prematurely. On discovering him on the premises, Mrs Liddell said, 'How sorry you must be to see us, Mr. Ruskin!' 'I never was more so,' Ruskin replied. The socially awkward Ruskin was still more sorry a day or two later, when this story was related to the guests at a dinner he was attending at the Christ Church Deanery. The Prince and Princess of Wales were guests of honour, and, as a measure of just how far the story had spread, the narrator, 'perfect in every detail', was Benjamin Disraeli!

John Ruskin's role as the girls' teacher appears to be captured in 'The Mock Turtle's Story' in *Looking-Glass*, when the Turtle talks about his education in 'reeling and writhing' (i.e. reading and writing). He says, 'The Drawling-master was an old conger-eel that used to come once a week: *he* taught us Drawling, Stretching, and Fainting in Coils' (i.e. drawing, sketching, and painting in oils). †

---

* Rhoda was Alice's younger sister (1859–1949).
† Alice evidently learned well. She became an accomplished artist, and her skill as a wood-carver is displayed in Osney's church of St Frideswide, showing Oxford's patron saint arriving at Binsey by boat (see page 29).

5

FOLLY BRIDGE

In his article for *Cornhill Magazine,* Alice's son, Caryl Hargreaves, asked his readers to imagine Carroll and Robinson Duckworth escorting the three Liddell girls from Christ Church 'down to Salter's, where the rowing boats are kept, and watch them choose a nice roomy boat, and plenty of comfortable cushions'. Salter Brothers have been the dominant influence on the river at Folly Bridge, probable site of the original Oxen-ford across the Thames, since 1870, the year when they took over the business of local rival, Thomas Hall. Established in 1858, Salters', which built boats as well as hiring them, initially operated from the building which now accommodates The Head of the River pub.* Hall's, on the island opposite, also offered boats for hire, but frequent mentions in Oxford novels suggest that they catered more for competitive oarsmen, and, given their more convenient location, that Salters' would indeed have been Carroll's preferred choice.† Alice's own recollections in the

---

* 'Head of the River' is the term applied to the winning boat at the annual inter-college Eights' Week races (see page 69). The former warehouse was built in 1835/36.

† In *Three Men in a Boat* (1889), Jerome K. Jerome relates how he once pre-arranged the hire in Oxford of a double sculling skiff. At this date, Salters' are almost certain to be the firm which reserved for him the *Pride of the Thames,* which despite its encouraging name turned out to be 'an antediluvian chunk of wood that looked as though it had recently been dug out of somewhere, and dug out carelessly, so as to have been unnecessarily damaged in the process'.

38 *Alice in Waterland: Folly Bridge*

same *Cornhill* article certainly support the idea that they did hire a boat, rather than using one owned by the college:

In the usual way, after we had chosen our boat with great care, we three children were stowed away in the stern, and Mr Dodgson took the stroke oar. A pair of sculls was always laid in the boat for us little girls to handle when being taught to row by our indulgent host. He succeeded in teaching us in the course of these excursions, and it proved an unending joy to us. When we had learned enough to manage the oars, we were allowed to take our turn at them, while the two men watched and instructed us.

Alice revealed too who the second adult normally was: 'His brother occasionally took an oar in the merry party, but our most usual fifth was Mr Duckworth, who sang well.'

A short walk from Folly Bridge in the direction of Oxford lies Floyd's Row. This is now a side-entrance to Oxford Police Station, but in the nineteenth century it was a cul-de-sac of 26 terraced houses, ending at a branch of the Thames called the Trill Mill Stream. The 1861 and 1871 Censuses show that James and Elizabeth Prickett, the parents of Alice's governess Mary Prickett, lived at No. 12 (see Appendix 1).

11. (OPPOSITE) John and Stephen Salter's premises at Folly Bridge, probably early 1870s, as Stephen Salter retired in 1875. The lock (left) was removed in 1884, as part of the same flood-prevention scheme which saw the canalisation of the River Cherwell's confluence with the Thames (see page 63). On the far (Oxfordshire) bank of the Thames is the building which the two Salter brothers first occupied in 1858, now The Head of the River public house, next to which the Trill Mill Stream (out of picture) flows into the Thames. (*The Bodleian Library, University of Oxford MS Top. Oxon. d493 fol29*)

12. The two images which illustrate
the chapter in *Looking-Glass* called
'Wool and Water'. The interior of the
real shop at 83 St Aldate's is the reverse
of that in John Tenniel's images, as befits
a 'looking-glass' view. The real Alice
Liddell had dark hair and a fringe
(see pages 43 & 72); Tenniel chose to give
his 'Alice' a look made fashionable
by the Pre-Raphaelite movement.

6

ALICE'S SHOP

A little farther into town, on the western side of St Aldate's, is a building which illustrates a 'Waterland' theme as much as any lying closer to the actual river. This is No. 83 St Aldate's, probably the very shop drawn by Tenniel to illustrate the chapter in *Looking-Glass* called 'Wool and Water'. This is an apparently illogical episode, with a sheep as a shopkeeper and an unexplained transformation of the scene from the shop interior to a river.

The character of the Sheep would seem to have been a shared joke between Alice and Carroll, at the expense of the shopkeeper's wife, who either sounded or looked to them like a sheep.* But why the sudden transformation from a shop to a river? A logical explanation derives from Oxford's age-old vulnerability to flooding. Many are the historical instances of inhabitants of the low-lying parts of the city having to resort to their upper rooms in haste, and being obliged to move from house to house by boat.† No. 83 St Aldate's was unlikely to be affected in normal years, but in December 1852, Carroll's second winter in Oxford, the behaviour of the river was not

---

* The shopkeepers at No. 83 St Aldate's in 1861 and 1871 were John (born c. 1798) and Mary (born c. 1802) Millin. In 1851 the pair had traded as greengrocers, possibly from the same premises.
† The earliest example of Oxford as a setting for fiction, Chaucer's *The Miller's Tale*, plays on this theme, with a focus on Osney.

at all normal. The *Illustrated London News* of 4 December reported exceptional flooding, several drownings, and the need to use boats to move passengers to and from the railway station: 'The Cherwell and Isis* are, in extent, more like seas than rivers. All descriptions of property were to be seen floating down the waters, and carcasses of sheep, pigs, and horses, were seen lying in many parts of the country where the water has been drained off.'

This event is incorporated into the novel *The Adventures of Mr. Verdant Green*, set initially in 1852, by Rev. Edward Bradley (1827–89), writing under the name of 'Cuthbert Bede'. Lewis Carroll was a freshman of almost the same vintage as the fictional Verdant Green, a coincidence which makes the novel's descriptions especially pertinent. The floods occurred in Green's second term, but Carroll's sixth.

> One of those inundations occurred to which Oxford is so liable, and the meadow-land to the south and west of the city was covered by the flood. Boats plied to and from the railway station in place of omnibuses; ... the Isis was amplified to the width of Christ Church meadows; the Broad Walk had a peep at itself upside down in the glassy mirror; the windings of the Cherwell could only be traced by the trees on its banks. There was 'Water, water everywhere'; and a disagreeable quantity of it too, as those Christ Church men whose ground-floor rooms were towards the meadows soon discovered.†

---

* The Isis is an alternative name for the Thames, applied in general only as it flows past Oxford. It has no clear historical or geographical derivation, seeming to be merely an Oxford affectation. Carroll himself remains neutral on the matter, always referring simply to 'the river'.

† The rooms in question would have pre-dated the Meadow Buildings which comprise the current southern entrance to the college. These were constructed in 1862–65, during the tenure of Dean Liddell. At the same time Liddell oversaw improvements to the 'Broad Walk', which leads down to the Cherwell River, following a design still apparent today.

It seems certain that if water reached as far as Christ Church, then 'Alice's Shop', in a slight depression in the nearby road (and with its floor below street level), would have been flooded that winter, and probably on other occasions to which Carroll would have been witness. A photograph (Cotsen Collection, Princeton, USA) taken by Carroll's friend Reginald Southey (see page 50) in 1855 shows the flooded Broad Walk much as it is described in *Verdant Green*, for instance, and the summer of 1860 was another time when the Oxford area suffered several weeks of extensive flooding. Alice's 'plaintive tone' when saying 'Things flow about so here!' surely echoed the laments of many a flood-affected Oxford resident of the time!

13. Sketch of Alice Liddell, aged eight, copied by Carroll from the photograph on page 72.

14. 'The Inundation of Christchurch Meadows, Oxford' from the *Illustrated London News* of 4 December 1852. The central spire is Tom Tower, which marks the entrance to Christ Church from St Aldate's.

TEXT

Alice enters the Shop in 'Wool and Water' after following the White Queen across one of the little brooks which represent the horizontal edges of the squares on the chessboard (hedges being the vertical edges). The Queen transmogrifies into the Sheep, who is behind the counter, and, somewhat creepily, busy knitting.

'Can you row?' the Sheep asked, handing her a pair of knitting-needles as she spoke.

'Yes, a little – but not on land – and not with needles –' Alice was beginning to say, when suddenly the needles turned into oars in her hands, and she found they were in a little boat, gliding along between banks: so there was nothing for it but to do her best.

'Feather!' cried the Sheep, as she took up another pair of needles.

The Sheep repeats the word several more times.*

'*Why* do you say "Feather" so often?' Alice asked at last, rather vexed. 'I'm not a bird!'

'You are,' said the Sheep: 'you're a little goose.'

This offended Alice a little, so there was no more conversation for a minute or two, while the boat glided gently

---

* In rowing, the feathering of oars is to turn the blades horizontal at the end of each pull, and move them forward again for the next pull by skimming the surface. In *Cornhill Magazine*, Alice commented: 'I can remember what hard work it was rowing upstream from Nuneham but this was nothing if we thought we were learning and getting on. It was a proud day when we could "feather our oars" properly.'

on, sometimes among beds of weeds (which made the oars stick fast in the water, worse than ever), and sometimes under trees, but always with the same tall river-banks frowning over their heads.'*

Later Alice spies some scented rushes.

'Please may we wait and pick some?' Alice pleaded. 'If you don't mind stopping the boat for a minute.'

'How am *I* to stop it?' said the Sheep. 'If you leave off rowing, it'll stop of itself.'

So the boat was left to drift down the stream as it would, till it glided gently in among the waving rushes. And then the little sleeves were carefully rolled up, and the little arms were plunged in elbow-deep, to get hold of the rushes a good long way down before breaking them off – and for a while Alice forgot all about the Sheep and the knitting, as she bent over the side of the boat, with just the ends of her tangled hair dipping into the water – while with bright eager eyes she caught at one bunch after another of the darling scented rushes.

'Wool and Water' ends back at the Shop. After a play on the word 'crab', another rowing term, the Sheep asks Alice if it is a crab that she wishes to buy. Put on the spot, she decides that it is an egg that she wants, which leads to the next chapter, called 'Humpty Dumpty', and Alice's progression over another brook to the next row of the chessboard.

---

* In fact, nowhere on the braided streams of the river between Godstow and Nuneham can the banks be said to be tall, except possibly below Osney Lock – although to a girl of Alice's age, they may often of course have appeared so.

7

TRILL MILL STREAM

When composing the preceding passage from 'Wool and Water', Carroll could have had in mind almost any of Oxford's myriad streams. Yet the one that flows closest to the Shop itself, the Trill Mill Stream, is an unlikely candidate – even though in real life it would certainly have been a contributory factor to any local flooding. Despite its attractive name, the Trill Mill Stream was not at all the sort of waterway that would have tempted a young girl to plunge in her little arms or dip her tangled hair. The reason was the Stream's notorious reputation for pollution.

Alice's son, Caryl Hargreaves, alludes to this in his introduction to Alice's recollections in *Cornhill Magazine*. Inviting the reader to accompany the three girls from Christ Church to the river (see page 37), Hargreaves wrote that 'the way down to the river and to the boats was alongside the Till [sic] Mill stream, an evil-smelling and altogether undesirable approach to the river'.

Indeed it was! The notoriety of the Trill Mill Stream's polluted waters earned it the ironic nickname 'Pactolus', in erudite contrast to the stream of that name in the Greek myth of King Midas, who turned everything that he touched into gold. In *Curiosities of Natural History*, Francis Buckland wrote in 1859 that 'the modern Pactolus does not contain gold but something convertible into gold, if used by the farmer as manure'.

To tackle this problem, the stream was culverted in 1863, causing it to disappear near Oxford Castle and to re-emerge in Christ Church's grounds (now comprising the Memorial Gardens, which were laid out in 1926 – see Appendix 2).* Evidently the impact was not immediate. In the September 1871 issue of the short-lived Oxford journal *Dark Blue,* the stream was decried as one 'whose bottom contains ten feet of seething odour, the surface of which is so vile, that it does but disgust, defile and infect a whole population'. The problem was not confined to the Trill Mill Stream, however. The article continues:

> Nasty, very nasty, is every branch of the Cherwell, dead-doggy and befouled is Isis, venomous is Pactolus; crawling with insect life is the railway-cutting pond which supplies Oxford with water, but the gas works, in respect of stink, are – simply — .

No words, evidently, were adequate – or at least, none fit for Victorian sensibilities! One can see why Dean Liddell approved a new, wide, tree-lined avenue down to the Thames in 1872 (the one still used, known as the 'Long Walk'), as an alternative to the old path next to the sickly Trill Mill Stream (on the opposite side of which was Floyd's Row, where Mary Prickett's parents lived).

---

* It seems likely that Dean Liddell would have been instrumental in this measure. He introduced many changes to Christ Church after his appointment in 1855, not all of them within the confines of the college buildings. *The Alice Companion* notes: 'Sewers were one of his abiding concerns; one German professor, seeking audience with the famous lexicographer, was told that Henry Liddell had "gone down the drain" – and could be found underground beneath Christ Church meadow.'

8

CHRIST CHURCH MEADOW

15. 'A Punting Scene by the Christ Church Meadows Oxford' from *College Life* by Edward Bradley (c1850). Tom Tower and Christ Church Cathedral are in the background.

Diary

25 FEB. 1856

First afternoon of the torpids. Frank and I went down to see them and fell in with the Liddell party. (Mrs. L., her sister, and the two eldest children). We bumped University, and are now second. *

6 MARCH 1856

Made friends with little Harry Liddell, (whom I first spoke to down at the boats last week): he is certainly the handsomest boy I ever saw.

25 APRIL 1856 (Fri.)

Went over with Southey† in the afternoon to the Deanery, to try and take a photograph of the Cathedral: both attempts proved failures. The three little girls were in the garden most of the time, and we became excellent friends: we tried to group them in the foreground of the picture, but they were not patient sitters. I mark this day with a white stone.

---

* The party consisted of Alice's mother, Lorina Hannah Reeve (1826–1910), who married Henry Liddell in 1846; Mrs Pleasance Elizabeth Fellows; Harry (1847–1911), and Ina (1849–1930). This day marked Carroll's first meeting with Dean Liddell's immediate family, but he had already encountered some distant cousins by chance the previous year, in Whitburn. The two days when he conversed with seven-year-old Frederica Liddell – 4 and 21 September 1855 – were the earliest to which Carroll applied the term 'white stone day', denoting a date of especial significance. For an explanation of 'bumping' see page 69.

† Reginald Southey (1835–99), a Christ Church graduate who encouraged Carroll's interest in photography. At the time Ina was nearly seven, Alice nearly four, and Edith two. Carroll took delivery of the first camera of his own on 1 May 1856. An intriguing character in the 1850s novel *Verdant Green* is Fanny Bouncer, described as 'a clever proficient in the fascinating art of photography', and capable both of taking the photographs and producing calotypes using her own chemicals – much as Carroll did, using the wet collodion method.

22 OCT. 1856

Fell in with Harry and Ina Liddell down in the meadow, and took them up to see my book of photographs.

3 NOV. 1856 (Mon.)

Met Miss Prickett, the governess, at the Deanery, walking with Ina, and settled I would come over on Wednesday morning, if it is fine.

5 NOV. 1856 (Wed.)

The morning was fair, and I took my camera over to the Deanery, just in time to see the whole party (except Edith) set off with the carriage and ponies, a disappointment for me, as it is the last vacant morning I shall have in the term. However, I must manage to clear another morning.

29 JAN. 1857

Arranged with Miss Prickett for Harry Liddell to come to me three days a week … to learn sums.

5 FEB. 1857

Walking in the afternoon I fell in with Ina Liddell and the governess, and returned with them to the Deanery, where I spent about an hour with the young party in the schoolroom.

22 FEB. 1857 (Sun.)

Met (as usual) Harry and Ina in the meadow, and took Harry with me into chapel.

12 APRIL 1857 (Sun.)

In the afternoon I walked in the meadow (as usual) with Harry, Ina, and the governess, and took Harry to chapel.

27 MAY 1857

Took Harry down to see the races in the evening. We went on to the barge for a short time, but I did not like staying long, as some of the men there were very undesirable acquaintances for him.

2 AUG. 1862 (Sat.)

Mrs. Brodie brought her children over to be photographed in the morning ... after which Margaret and Ida* came down again to go, with the Liddells, Harcourt, and myself, on the water. Then back to croquêt at the Deanery, and Harcourt and I went there again after dinner to escort the Brodies home, the Liddells also insisting on walking there and back with us.

29 APRIL 1863

There is no variety in my life to record just now <u>except</u> meetings with the Liddells, the record of which has become almost continuous. I walked with them in the meadow this morning.

6 MAY 1864

Walked on the other side of the river, and met Ina, Alice and Edith, with Miss Prickett: we inspected the new 'grand stand' intended for spectators of the boat-races. Went down to the races, and saw Ch. Ch. bump Magdalen.

---

* Two of the daughters of the chemist Benjamin Collins Brodie (1817–80).

CHRIST CHURCH MEADOW

However unpleasant the waters of the Trill Mill Stream really were, Christ Church Meadow itself, of which the Stream marked its western extent, was still a supremely attractive place to take walks. Carroll's diary has many references to walking here with the Liddell girls. Usually he met them in passing, rather than by arrangement – although their routine *does* seem to have been fairly predictable. Alice (*Cornhill Magazine*): 'We used always to go out for about an hour's walk before luncheon at one o'clock. Sometimes we went out towards Bagley Wood, sometimes round Christ Church meadows, sometimes towards North Oxford, which was then open fields.' Mary Prickett, the governess, would of course always accompany them.

Occasionally Carroll mentions more distant encounters, notably out towards the villages of Hinksey.* Inevitably these walks would mean crossing the many small streams derived from the braiding of the Thames on the Berkshire side of its main course. It is noticeable that the only walks of which Carroll makes any mention in the creatively important years of 1862–64 are those in which he encounters the Liddells, even though, as an avid walker all his life, he no doubt went on many, many more. He seems glumly aware of this pattern, writing

---

* See page 61. John Ruskin particularly liked the walk to North Hinksey, and arranged for a group of his students (including Oscar Wilde) to repair the road there with him in 1874, after seeking the permission of the landowner, Edward Harcourt. Sadly, after all their efforts, a surveyor felt unable to summon any greater enthusiasm for 'Ruskin's Road' than to say, 'the young men have done no mischief to speak of' (*The Oxford Book of Oxford*, Jan Morris, 1978)!

on 29 April 1863: 'There is no variety in my life to record just now except meetings with the Liddells.'

Another regular walking companion of Alice was canine. A 'special pleasure was to be allowed to take Rover out for a walk. Rover was a retriever belonging to a well-known Oxford tailor, called Randall, who lived in a house built on arches over the Isis, which he christened Grandpont' (*Cornhill*). This house (the name deriving from the original Norman name for Folly Bridge) is described in *Verdant Green* as 'that eccentric mansion … possessing in the place of cellars an ingenious system of small rivers'. Randall was a hatter (see Appendix 3) as well

16. Grandpont House, with its 'ingenious system of small rivers' instead of cellars. The home of Alderman Thomas Randall (and his dog Rover!) when Alice Liddell was a girl, photographed by Henry Taunt (1900). (*Images & Voices, Oxfordshire County Council*)

as a tailor, and in 1855 the Oxford University Boat Club purchased silk hats from him, at a time when sartorial elegance on the water still counted for much (Sherriff, 2003).

Carroll himself 'dressed down' on his river trips: 'Mr. Dodgson always wore black clergymen's clothes in Oxford, but, when he took us out on the river, he used to wear white flannel trousers. He also replaced his black top-hat by a hard white straw hat on these occasions, but of course retained his black boots, because in those days white tennis shoes had never been heard of. He always carried himself upright, almost more than upright, as if he had swallowed a poker' (*Cornhill*).

In the middle of the nineteenth century, Christ Church Meadow's river bank was lined with large, ornate barges belonging to various colleges (see Appendix 4). These imposing vessels had a dual purpose: to provide somewhere for rowers to change, and for spectators to view the regular races held on this stretch of the river. The scene in about 1857 is described by the Halls in *The Book of the Thames*. Of the Exeter College and newly purchased University Boat Club barges they wrote:

> Both are of costly workmanship, the latter being somewhat sombre in style when we saw it, but now, as we learn, richly decorated with colour, and displaying the armorial bearings of all the colleges: the former still flaunting in scarlet and gold, although age and use have somewhat tarnished its brilliancy. These 'vessels' serve as floating club-houses, and are well supplied with newspapers, periodicals, and writing materials, and have dressing-rooms for members. They are not calculated for making voyages, and are rarely released from their moorings.

Cuthbert Bede's fictional hero Verdant Green frequented 'the floating reading-room of the University barge' in the early 1850s.

There he could study the news of the day, and

> look out upon the picturesque river with its moving life of eights and four-oars sweeping past with measured stroke. A great feature of the river picture, just about this time, was the crowd of newly introduced canoes; their occupants, in every variety of bright-coloured shirts and caps, flashing up and down a double paddle, the ends of which were painted in gay colours, or emblazoned with the owner's crest.

The novel also includes a description of the view across Christ Church Meadow:

> Through openings in the trees there were glimpses of grey old college-buildings; then came the walk along the banks, the Isis shining like molten silver, and fringed around with barges and boats; then another stretch of green meadows; then a cloud of steam from the railway-station; and a background of gently rising hills.[*]

It was at the three main rowing events of the academic year that the college barges really came into their own. The Torpid races were held early in the year, for the second-string crews. The major event, then and now, was Eights' Week, held in May, and so called because the crews consist of eight rowers. Inter-college rivalry was fierce, and the races always attracted a great number of spectators: townspeople as well as students. Nineteenth-century Oxford novelists were fond of including Eights' Week or the other major river event of the summer – the 'procession of boats' during Commemoration – in their plots. This was not just because of the descriptive opportunity offered

---

[*] The station referred to is Oxford's first, opened by the Great Western Railway Co. in 1844, on the south side of the Thames near Folly Bridge. It was superseded by a new station, near Oxford's current station, in October 1852.

by the excitement and colour of the day, but because the occasion enabled writers to introduce some romance into the storyline, with the arrival of female relatives in a city with a disproportionally large male population.

In *Tom Brown at Oxford,* Thomas Hughes* describes the procession of boats during a Commemoration of the early 1840s:

> The barges above and below the University barge, which occupied the post of honour, were also covered with ladies, and Christchurch Meadow swarmed with gay dresses and caps and gowns. On the opposite side the bank was lined with a crowd in holiday clothes, and the punts plied across without intermission loaded with people, until the groups stretched away down the towing path in an almost continuous line to the starting place. Then one after another the racing-boats, all painted and polished up for the occasion, with the college flags drooping at their sterns, put out and passed down to their stations, and the bands played, and the sun shone his best.

In *Verdant Green* the influx of femininity is stressed rather more: 'How a few flounces and bright girlish smiles can change the aspect of the sternest homes of knowledge! How sunlight can be brought into the gloomiest nooks of learning by the beams that irradiate happy girlish faces.'

It is rare to find a hero of a nineteenth-century Oxford novel who was not in some way responsible for a triumph by his college's boating crew. Carroll, although he enjoyed rowing for pleasure, seems not to

---

* Thomas Hughes (1822–96) was at Oxford in the early 1840s, and was an excellent oarsman. His brother George was still more proficient, and rowed in a famous inter-varsity race against Cambridge in 1843 which is said to have marked the elevation of the sport to *the* predominant University recreation (see Appendix 5). Both Hughes brothers attended Rugby school (the setting for *Tom Brown's Schooldays*) a few years prior to Carroll, who was a pupil there between 1846 and 1849.

Another Rugby old boy was Matthew Arnold (1822–88), who penned the famous 'dreaming spires' description of Oxford in his 1867 poem *Thyrsis.*

have been especially interested in these competitive events. Certainly there are few references to them in his diaries. However, the racing did provide Carroll with his first opportunity for social interaction with the Liddells, when he talked to Mrs Liddell, her sister, and the two eldest children, Harry and Ina, at the Torpid races of February 1856. Two weeks later he met Harry again, and subsequently took him out on the river several times (and again the following summer of 1857). During the same Spring, on 25 April 1856, Carroll first made the acquaintance of Alice, when he and Reginald Southey were taking photographs of Christ Church Cathedral.

The photographic sessions with the Liddells, almost as much as the boat trips, were a cue for more stories. Alice (*Cornhill*): 'We used to sit on the big sofa on each side of him, while he told us stories, illustrating them by pencil or ink drawings as he went along. When we were thoroughly happy and amused at his stories, he used to pose us, and expose the photos before the mood had passed.' In Collingwood's *Life and Letters*, Alice is quoted as saying: 'Another day, perhaps, the story would begin in the boat, and Mr Dodgson, in the middle of telling a thrilling adventure, would pretend to fall fast asleep, to our great dismay.'

9

RIVER CHERWELL

17. College barges line the bank of Christ Church Meadow, Folly Bridge is in the distance, and Grandpont House can be seen on the left in Henry Taunt's view (c1870) from the towpath on the south bank of the Thames. The River Cherwell joins the Thames just downstream of this point.
(*Images & Voices, Oxfordshire County Council*)

Diary

3 MARCH 1857

Went on the river with Skeffington and Wilfred.* We went about 5 miles up the Cherwell, just after clearing the rapids the bow-oar broke, and we turned homewards, after binding up the fracture with the painter in the best way we could.

18 APRIL 1857

Went up the Cherwell in a gig with Joyce (Senior) and Harry Liddell.

10 MARCH 1863

Edwin† and I went into the Broad Walk to see the three Deanery children plant three trees along the Cherwell, in memory of the day, each delivered a short speech over her tree 'long life to this tree, and may it prosper from this auspicious day', and they named them Alexandra, Albert, and Victoria. After the tree-planting we escorted the Liddells and Mrs. Reeve‡ to see the ox roasted whole near Worcester,§ which was <u>not</u> an exciting spectacle. At three was the last Torpid race, for which we went on to the barge, and of course met the Liddells again. After Hall we went to the Deanery for the children, and set out. We soon lost the others, and Alice and I with

---

* Carroll's brothers Skeffington Dodgson (1836–1919) and Wilfred Dodgson (1838–1914), both of whom studied at Christ Church.
† Carroll's youngest brother Edwin Dodgson (1846–1913).
‡ Mrs Lorina Reeve, née Farr (1794–1879), Alice's grandmother from Suffolk.
§ Meaning Worcester College, nicknamed 'Botany Bay' in *Verdant Green* on account of its remoteness from all the other colleges. The ox-roast was actually in Jericho (*Jackson's Oxford Journal*, 14 March 1863), which lies immediately to the north of Worcester College.

Edwin, took the round of all the principal streets in about two hours, bringing her home by half-past nine. The mob was dense, but well conducted. The fireworks abundant, and some of the illuminations very beautiful. It was delightful to see the thorough abandonment with which Alice enjoyed the whole thing.* The Wedding-day of the Prince of Wales I mark with a white stone.

20 MARCH 1863

Spent the morning, as usual, partly in Hall, and partly in the Broad Walk, where I had the company of Ina and Edith with Miss Prickett.

Took a second walk out towards Hinksey, and again fell in with the Liddells, with whom (after a race with Ina on the bridge over the reservoir) I walked back into Oxford.

22 APRIL 1863

Going through Ch. Ch. in the afternoon I met little Mary Norris, who told me of the flower-show going on in the new Exchange. I went in, and there fell in with Ina, Edith, and Miss Prickett (and also Lady Brodie and her five). I afterwards had a _very_ pleasant walk with them round by the two Hinkseys, going up on to the hill near Ferry Hinksey.

27 APRIL 1863

Walked towards Hinksey and fell in with Ina, Edith and governess, and went with them to our old cricket-ground, to see the militia drilled.

---

* The evening was one which was still etched in Alice's memory almost 70 years later. 'The crowd in the streets was very great, and I clung tightly to the hand of the strong man on either side of me. The colleges were all lit up, and the High Street was a mass of illuminations of all sorts and kinds' (*Cornhill Magazine*, July 1932).

18. 'Magdalen Tower and Bridge, From the Cherwell', from the 1855 University Almanac.
(The Bodleian Library, University of Oxford. G.A. Oxon. a.92)

62   *Alice in Waterland: River Cherwell*

RIVER CHERWELL

Almost all of the rowing trips recorded by Carroll were on the Thames. Only two outings on its tributary the River Cherwell are known, both in 1857 (and one of them with Harry Liddell). At the time, the Cherwell had only one navigable confluence with the Thames, flowing, as today, immediately alongside Christ Church Meadow. A smaller second outlet to the Thames was canalised in 1884, as a flood-prevention measure. This helped to re-define both the island now occupied by the boathouses (which replaced the picturesque college barges from 1939 onwards) and the much larger Aston's Eyot* downstream.

Apart from in 1857, Carroll's only other mention of the Cherwell came on Tuesday 10 March 1863. This was the day that the Prince of Wales (later King Edward VII) married Princess Alexandra of Denmark. As he often did, Carroll took a stroll that day along the Broad Walk, and came across the three Liddell girls planting elm saplings on the bank of the Cherwell in honour of the day.[†] Later on, Carroll joined the Liddells on the Christ Church barge to watch the Torpids, and in the evening he and his brother Edwin took Alice through the crowded streets to see the celebratory illuminations and fireworks.

----

* The word 'eyot' derives from the Old English for an island, or marshy bit of land – 'waterland', in fact, one might say! The 'ey' ending of so many place names bordering the river in Oxford – Medley, Binsey, Osney, Hinksey, and even 'Portmanheit' (the original name of Port Meadow) – demonstrates the defining influence of Oxford's myriad streams in dictating the pattern of human habitation.

† The girls' wishes of 'a long life' for their trees were partly met: they eventually succumbed to the Dutch Elm Disease which afflicted much of northern Europe in the 1970s.

A few months later, the newly wed royal couple stayed at Christ Church (where the Prince had been an undergraduate, commencing in 1859) when in Oxford to receive an honorary degree. It was an occasion which enthralled the entire city, both Town and Gown (that is, both the inhabitants of Oxford and the members of its University). *Jackson's Oxford Journal* was effusive, devoting nearly half of its entire news output of 20 June 1863 to the event. The Prince and Princess's first public engagement on arriving was an awards ceremony at Christ Church, where they were 'received by the Dean of Christ Church, with Mrs. Liddell and their family'.

This was Commemoration Week, so the next day, Wednesday 17 June, after playing croquet with the Liddell girls in the afternoon, the Prince and Princess attended the procession of boats. *Jackson's* reported that

> [a] grand stand had been erected on the Berkshire side of the river to accommodate upwards of a thousand members and friends of the University Boat Club, both banks of the Isis were thronged with spectators; barges and rafts were eagerly scrambled for, and numberless boats of every description speckled the water.

The royal couple left the Deanery about 6pm, and at Folly Bridge 'embarked in a very handsome boat, stylishly fitted up, built expressly for the occasion by Messrs. Salter, by order of the University Boat Club'. In this vessel the royal couple were rowed as far as the confluence with the Cherwell, then back to take pride of place on the University barge. Then came the procession, described in the *Illustrated London News* of 27 June. As 'Head of the River', the Trinity College boat, after

> flying over the water as silently and quickly as a bird, stopped in its own length before the Royal barge, that the boats of all the other

colleges might do homage to their supremacy and past year's triumph over them. This they did in the usual manner as they came by in long procession, tossing their oars in honour of Trinity, and then waving their hats and cheering in honour of the Princess, who seemed deeply amused and interested in the whole proceeding.

Then 'the whole long file of boats swept under Folly Bridge, and, turning there, came back again in procession two and two abreast'. Evidently, it was common during the Commemoration procession for some kind of mishap to occur, and if it did not, one was contrived,

19. 'The Oxford Commemoration: the Procession of Boats' from the *Illustrated London News* of 27 June 1863. The Trinity College boat is stationed in front of the University barge (middle right), from which the Prince and Princess of Wales watched the proceedings. The crew hold their oars aloft, reciprocating the salute of each boat as it passes in the direction of Folly Bridge (in the distance) before returning downstream.

for the amusement of the spectators. Consequently, Balliol's Torpid crew's boat obligingly turned over immediately in front of the Prince and Princess. In addition, according to *Jackson's,* 'there were several other duckings, which excited great merriment, and one of the rafts, through unequal weight on one end, was partially capsized, with some effect on the nerves of the female portion of its crew'.

The next afternoon, Thursday 18 June, the royal couple departed by train, and 'having taken a cordial leave of the Dean, Mrs. Liddell, and their children, the special train moved off, amidst hearty cheers'. *Jackson's* concluded: 'And thus ended a Commemoration the like of which Oxford has never seen before and which none, of this generation at least, can expect to see again.'

The overturning of a boat on these occasions is captured in *Tom Brown at Oxford.* Having triumphed as 'Head of the River' in the May Eights, the fictional St Ambrose College boat, of which Tom is a crew member, is stationed (as Trinity's really was in 1863) to receive the acknowledgements of the other 23 eight-oars in the procession, 'with their flags flying, and all the crews in uniform'. Then 'the boats passed up one by one; and, as each came opposite to the St. Ambrose boat, the crews tossed their oars and cheered, and the St. Ambrose crew tossed their oars and cheered in return, and the whole ceremony went off in triumph.' However, one of the Torpids – boats which contain 'the refuse of the rowing men – generally awkward or very young oarsmen' – fares less well. The boat, 'having sustained her crew gallantly to the saluting point, and allowed them to get their oars fairly in the air, proceeded gravely to turn over on her side, and shoot them out into the stream'.

10

IFFLEY LOCK

20. 'Starting the Favorite' from *Reminiscences of Oxford Varsity Life* (anon) showing a rowing eight at the start above Iffley Lock. The date is not certain, but the publishers (T. & G. Shrimpton, Oxford) traded by this name from before 1852 until 1871. Morrell's (not Morells) Brewery was Oxford's longest lasting, closing in 1998. 'Entire' was a popular, strong beer similar to porter.

Diary

26 MAY 1862

Went down the river with Southey, taking Ina, Alice, and Edith with us: we only went to Iffley. Even then it was hard work rowing up again, the stream is so strong.*

30 JUNE 1862

Went with Atkinson to the boat procession then he sculled me down to Iffley.

5 MAY 1863

Walked in the afternoon with the trio and governess by the river side to a little below Iffley.

25 MAY 1863

Fell in with the children by the Botanical Gardens, and walked with them, a very merry party, round by Iffley.

---

* This was Alice's first known river trip. She had certainly been on other excursions before this, recalling four or five trips per summer in her *Cornhill Magazine* article, but because Carroll's diaries for the period April 1858 to May 1862 are missing, there is no actual record.

IFFLEY LOCK

The first river lock downstream of Christ Church is at Iffley. This was the destination on the first outing that Alice is known to have taken on the river with Carroll, on 26 May 1862 – although she undoubtedly did accompany him on earlier, unrecorded, trips too. Despite the time of year, conditions appear to have been less than perfect, judging by Carroll's unusual reference to finding the rowing 'hard work'.

The bank above Iffley Lock is where the Torpid and Eights' races commence, overlooked by the Isis Tavern (now Isis Farmhouse), which was converted from a farm building in 1842. The starting order of the different college boats, one behind the other along the bank, is pre-defined by their ranking the previous year. The object is to catch, or 'bump', the boat immediately in front before it reaches the finish near Folly Bridge. If successful, the two boats' positions are reversed in the next heat, meaning that over the course of the week the faster crews move up the rankings, until on the final day the fastest crew of all is named 'Head of the River'.

Thomas Hughes, in *Tom Brown at Oxford*, described the overall scene during Eights' Week from the informed perspective of a former winning competitor.

> The banks of the river were crowded; and the punts plied rapidly backwards and forwards, carrying loads of men over to the Berkshire side. The university barge, and all the other barges, were decked with flags, and the band was playing lively airs.

Small groups of gownsmen were scattered along the bank in Christchurch meadow, chiefly dons, who were really interested in the races, but, at this time of day, seldom liked to display enthusiasm enough to cross the water and go down to the starting-place. These sombre groups were lighted up here and there by the dresses of a few ladies, who were walking up and down, and watching the boats.

Iffley is significant among Thames locks in that it was the location (with Sandford and another near Abingdon) of one of the first three seventeenth-century chamber locks (i.e. with two gates, as opposed to the single gate of the much more common 'flash' locks) on the whole Thames. Carroll would have passed through it on all of his rowing trips down the river – to Rose Island, Sandford, and Nuneham.

Iffley is also the location of a rare indication that Alice Liddell's enthusiasm for rowing lasted beyond her childhood years. Queen Victoria's youngest son, Prince Leopold (1853–1884), followed his brother, Edward the Prince of Wales, to Christ Church in 1872, and studied there for three years. Colin Gordon, in *Beyond the Looking Glass,* describes

> a scrap of paper, part of Alice's pencilled notes for her recollections at eighty. It ... recalls an episode on a boating trip with the prince to Iffley, where Alice accidentally gave the prince a black eye with her oar. Leopold wondered what he would say to the Queen, who, thought Alice, would not have approved of such informal messing about in boats with young ladies. Anyway, Alice concluded, 'I was never ordered to be beheaded'.

Alice's final comment is of course a reference to *Wonderland*'s Queen of Hearts, whose favourite expression was 'Off with his/her/their head(s)!'

21. (OPPOSITE) 'A Picnic to Nuneham: in Iffley Lock' from *The Graphic* 3 June 1882.

22. The photograph of Alice, aged eight, which Carroll had affixed at the end of the manuscript of 'Alice's Adventures under Ground' (over the sketch of it on page 43).

11

ROSE ISLAND

23. The Swan Inn on Rose (or Kennington, also called St Michael's) Island, the destination of Carroll's probable first boat outing with Ina Liddell on 5 June 1856. The photograph was taken by Henry Taunt in 1885.

(Images & Voices, Oxfordshire County Council)

Diary

5 JUNE 1856

From half past four to seven, Frank and I made a boating excursion with Harry and Ina: the latter, much to my surprise, having got permission from the Dean to come. We went down to the island, and made a kind of picnic there, taking biscuits with us, and buying gingerbeer and lemonade there. Harry as before rowed stroke most of the way, and fortunately, considering the wild spirits of the children, we got home without accident, having attracted by our remarkable crew a good deal of attention from almost every one we met. Mark this day, Annalist, not only with a white stone, but as altogether dies mirabilis. **

1 MAY 1863

At half-past two Duckworth and I went down the river with the three Liddells and Miss Prickett. We did not get quite down to the island, but rowed up and down, varying the performance by songs from the children.

---

* This appears to be Ina's first outing. The 14th was on 6 August 1862 (see page 5).

ROSE ISLAND

Rose Island is on a bend in the river just below the railway bridge known as 'Kennington Viaduct'. Work was begun on this bridge, carrying the line to the Oxfordshire town of Thame, in 1863, and was completed by the end of 1864, its progress no doubt providing a considerable additional talking-point for any river travellers at the time. The line gained later importance as a feeder for the car works at Cowley, established by William Morris, later Lord Nuffield, in 1913.

The house on Rose Island was formerly a pub called The Swan Inn. This was the destination on what seems to have been the first ever river trip that Carroll made with any of the Liddell girls, on 5 June 1856. Evidently to Carroll's very great surprise (and delight, marking the day as exceptional even beyond a 'white stone' designation), he was permitted to take Ina, soon after her seventh birthday, and her brother Harry down to the island, where they bought gingerbeer and lemonade, to add to the biscuits that Carroll had brought with him. Later on he would be better prepared. Alice observed: 'He always brought out with him a large basket full of cakes, and a kettle which we used to boil under a haycock if we could find one' (*Cornhill Magazine*).

MAP 4

SANDFORD TO NUNEHAM

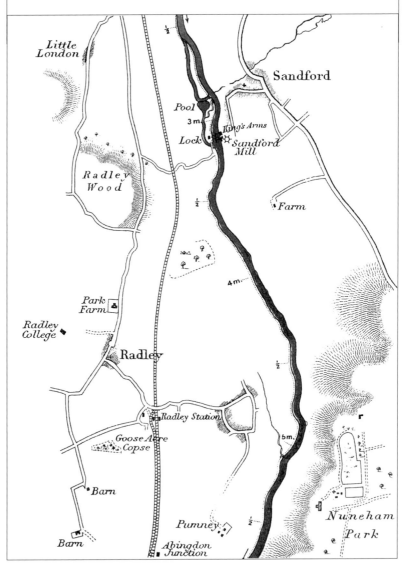

Source: Henry Taunt's *New Map of the River Thames* (ed. 3) 1879, surveyed 1878.

12

SANDFORD-ON-THAMES

24. 'Sandford Mill' from Alfred Rimmer's *Pleasant Spots Around Oxford* (1878).

Diary

6 MARCH 1855

Collyns, Liddon, and I went down as far as Sandford in an outriggered-gig.

27 APRIL 1855

Down the river with Liddon, the first time this term.

3 JUNE 1856

Spent the morning at the Deanery, photographing the children. In the afternoon went with Liddon to the Horticultural Show in Worcester Gardens. Afterwards Frank and I, with Harry Liddell, went down to Sandford in a gig. We rowed with sculls down with Harry as stroke, and he steered back.

8 MAY 1857

Went down the river as far as Sandford with Frank and Harry Liddell.

26 MAY 1857

Down the river with Joyce and Harry Liddell.

24 MARCH 1858

Down the river as far as Sandford in a gig with Tyrwhitt.

17 JUNE 1862 (Tues.)

Expedition to Nuneham. Duckworth (of Trinity) and Ina, Alice, and Edith came with us. We set out about $12^{1}/_{2}$ and got to Nuneham about 2: dined there, then walked in the park, and set off for home about $4^{1}/_{2}$. About a mile above Nuneham heavy rain came on, and after bearing it a short time I settled that we had better leave the boat and walk: three miles of this drenched us all pretty well. I went on first with the children, as they could walk much faster than Elizabeth, and took them to the only house I knew in Sandford, Mrs. Boughton's, where Ranken lodges. I left them with her to get their clothes dried, and went off to find a vehicle, but none was to be had there, so on the others arriving, Duckworth and I walked on to Iffley, whence we sent them a fly.*

13 JULY 1863

In the afternoon Kitchin† and I rowed down to the lock at Sandford and back.

---

* William Henry Ranken (1832–1920) was non-resident vicar of Sandford. Carroll preached evensong at Sandford Church on 8 June 1862, his first ever recorded sermon.
† George William Kitchin (1827–1912), a Christ Church undergraduate between 1846 and 1850, a lecturer from 1861 to 1863, and author of *Ruskin in Oxford* (1904).

SANDFORD-ON-THAMES

The episode of 'The Pool of Tears' in *Wonderland* was mainly inspired by what happened in Sandford on a rowing trip to Nuneham on Tuesday 17 June 1862. The party that afternoon was an unusually large one. Carroll and the three girls were joined by Robinson Duckworth, apparently for the first time, and two of Carroll's sisters. At least, that is what Alice recalled; Carroll is not specific about how many of his three visitors that week (his Aunt Lucy Lutwidge, and sisters Fanny and Elizabeth – see page 30) actually came in the boat. Soon after they had set off upstream for the journey home from Nuneham, it poured with rain. They abandoned the boat, then walked (three miles, Carroll says) to the village of Sandford, about a third of a mile from the lock, where the women and girls sheltered at the only house Carroll was familiar with there: the home of the schoolteacher, Mrs Boughton.* Carroll and Duckworth then walked to Iffley, and sent transport back for the women and girls.

Alice's own recollection of the day in *Cornhill Magazine* (mistakenly she recalled that they abandoned the boat at Iffley) suggests that it was not only the rain which put a dampener on this particular excursion: Carroll's sisters, she thought, were

---

* Carroll makes no allusion to the school; it is the 1861 Census which reveals that Mary Boughton was the Sandford schoolteacher, living at the school house.

rather stout, and one might have expected that, with such a load in it, the boat would have been swamped. However, it was not the river that swamped us but the rain. It came on to pour so hard that we had to land at Iffley, and after trying to dry the Misses Dodgson at a fire, we drove home. This was a serious party, no stories nor singing: we were awed by the 'old ladies', for though they can only have been in their twenties, they appeared dreadfully old to us.

The downpour of rain, occurring only a few weeks before the all-important trip to Godstow on 4 July, is commemorated in *Wonderland* by way of Alice's tears, which are so copious that several animals are in danger of drowning in the salty pool. Some of these animals are clearly identified: the Dodo (as an abbreviation of Dodgson) is Carroll, the Duck is Duckworth, and the Lory and Eaglet represent Lorina (Ina) and Edith. This episode also features in *Under Ground*, which Carroll illustrated himself. Both his and Tenniel's depictions of the scene include 'several other curious creatures', which may have been meant to represent some characteristic of Dodgson's sisters, though this is far from clear. A monkey is apparent in both men's artwork, however, at a time when Darwin's theories on evolution (following the publication of *On the Origin of Species* in 1859) were a matter of great topical debate. It could also be that the comment of the White Queen in the chapter called 'Queen Alice' in *Looking-Glass* – 'We had *such* a thunderstorm last Tuesday' – harks back to this day.

In the nineteenth century there was a productive paper mill at Sandford Lock, with an adjacent inn called (as it still is) The King's Arms. This was a popular spot for rowers, both casual and competitive, to stop off for refreshments, or to play skittles or quoits, and it features affectionately in a number of Oxford novels and memoirs.

Just upstream of Sandford Lock is a large overflow weir, known in Oxford as a 'lasher'. It has a mournful past, having claimed the lives of at least five Christ Church scholars. Among these were William Gaisford, the son of Thomas Gaisford (1779–1855), Henry Liddell's predecessor as Dean, who drowned here in June 1843, and Michael Llewellyn Davies in May 1921.*

25. Lewis Carroll's illustration of 'The Pool of Tears' from the original handwritten manuscript of 'Alice's Adventures under Ground', published in facsimile in 1886.

---

* Michael Llewelyn Davies was the ward of J.M. Barrie, who composed *Peter Pan* (1904) for the benefit of Michael and his brothers. Another Christ Church death intimately connected with a classic children's book inspired by the Thames was that of Kenneth Grahame's son, Alastair, for whom *Wind in the Willows* (1908) had originally been written. He was killed by a train in 1920, while a Christ Church undergraduate. Kenneth Grahame (1859–1932) himself had attended a school adjacent to the canal in Oxford from 1868 to 1875, and is buried in Oxford's Holywell cemetery, having 'passed the river on the 6th of July 1932, leaving Childhood and Literature through him the more blest for all time'.

26. Tenniel's animals, dry again after running the Caucus-race in *Wonderland*, watch as the Dodo presents Alice with her own thimble as a prize.

TEXTS

In 'Down the Rabbit-hole', the first chapter of *Wonderland* (and of *Under Ground*), Alice has consumed the 'Eat Me' cake, and grown too large to get through the door to 'the loveliest garden you ever saw'. She starts to cry, 'shedding gallons of tears, until there was a large pool, about four inches deep, all round her, and reaching half way across the hall'.

She shrinks when she fans herself until she is only three inches tall.

> At this moment her foot slipped, and splash! She was up to her chin in salt water. Her first idea was that she had fallen into the sea: then she remembered that she was under ground, and she soon made out that it was the pool of tears that she had wept when she was nine feet high.

Alice converses with a mouse, which has also slipped into the pool. It departs hurriedly when Alice mentions her cat, Dinah. Meanwhile:

> It was high time to go, for the pool was getting quite full of birds and animals that had fallen into it. There was a Duck and a Dodo, a Lory and an Eaglet, and several other curious creatures. Alice led the way and the whole party swam to the shore.
>
> They were indeed a curious looking party that assembled on the bank – the birds with draggled feathers, the animals with their fur clinging close to them – all dripping wet, cross, and uncomfortable.

In *Wonderland* this episode concludes with everyone getting dry by running the Caucus-race. Carroll's original manuscript, printed in facsimile in 1887 as *Alice's Adventures under Ground*, adheres much more closely to the reality of the day which inspired it. The Dodo says, 'I know of a house near here, where we could get the young lady and the rest of the party dried', and then

> The whole party moved along the river bank, (for the pool had by this time begun to flow out of the hall, and the edge of it was fringed with rushes and forget-me-nots,) in a slow procession, the Dodo leading the way. After a time the Dodo became impatient, and, leaving the Duck to bring up the rest of the party, moved on at a quicker pace with Alice, the Lory, and the Eaglet, and soon brought them to a little cottage, and there they sat snugly by the fire, wrapped in blankets, until the rest of the party had arrived, and they were all dry again.

When Alice again mentions her cat, Dinah, the birds make a rapid exit. She says to herself:

> I do wish some of them had stayed a little longer! and I was getting to be such friends with them – really the Lory and I were almost like sisters! And so was that dear little Eaglet! And then the Duck and the Dodo! How nicely the Duck sang to us as we came along through the water: and if the Dodo hadn't known the way to that nice little cottage, I don't know when we should have got dry again.

MAP 5

NUNEHAM TO CLIFTON HAMPDEN

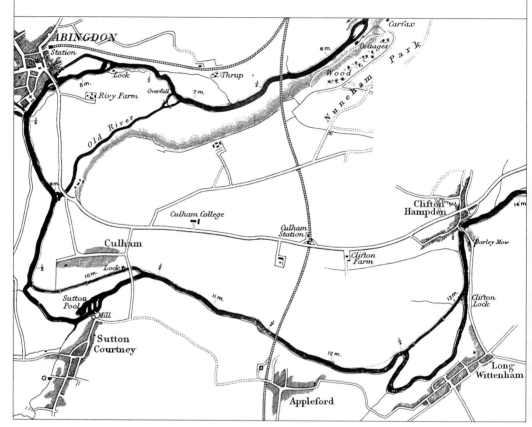

Source: Henry Taunt's *New Map of the River Thames* (ed. 3) 1879, surveyed 1878.

13

NUNEHAM

27. 'Nuneham Courteney' (probably mid-nineteenth century). In reality the house occupies a much more elevated position than the image implies, overlooking the landscaped parkland below, and enjoyed a view all the way to Oxford in one direction and Abingdon in the other. The area open to the public was downstream of this point.

Diary

7 MARCH 1855

Frank, Collyns, and I rowed to Nuneham, and called on Mr. Cooke, who was from home.

17 MAY 1857

Took Harry Liddell to chapel, and afterwards walked back with the children to the Deanery. I find to my great surprise that my notice of them is construed by some men into attentions to the governess, Miss Prickett.

It would be inconsiderate to the governess to give any further occasion for remarks of the sort. For this reason I shall avoid taking any public notice of the children in future.

17 APRIL 1863

Harry Liddell came to ask me to go with them down the river. Miss Prickett came (by Mrs. L's wish) with them. (I quite think that Ina is now so tall as to look odd without an escort.) I got Walter Scott to come and help to row, but he proved almost of no use. Harry sculled by himself, managed to be always in the way, and generally rather spoiled what would otherwise have been a very pleasant expedition.

9 JUNE 1863 (Tues.)

At three we (the children, Miss Prickett, and myself) set off down the river for Nuneham, reached it ten minutes past five, walked though Nuneham Park to Clifton Hampden* (1½ hours) where we had a sort of a meal (bread and butter, and ginger-beer,) and thence to the Culham Station, and back to Oxford by the 7.47. Afterwards I went over and had tea with the three children in the schoolroom, leaving at half-past nine. A very pleasant day, to be marked with a white stone.

25 JUNE 1863 (Thurs.)

About 10 o'clock Alice and Edith came over to my rooms to fetch me over to arrange about an expedition to Nuneham. It ended in our going down at three a party of ten, the Dean and Mrs. Liddell and the Dean's father, the three children and Rhoda, Harcourt, Lord Newry and myself. We took a four-oar, and the last three rowed all the way, the others taking it in turn to man the stroke-oar. We had tea under the trees at Nuneham, after which the rest drove home in the carriage (which met them in the park), while Ina, Alice, Edith, and I (mirabile dictu!) walked down to Abingdon-road station and so home by railway. A pleasant expedition with a <u>very</u> pleasant conclusion.

---

* Jerome K. Jerome (*Three Men in a Boat*, 1889) was much taken with Clifton Hampden, and especially its inn, and caught something of the essence of Carroll when outlining The Barley Mow's 'story-book appearance' and its 'still more once-upon-a-timeyfied' interior.

Diary

5 DEC. 1863

Ch. Ch. theatricals in Berners' rooms ... Mrs. Liddell and the children were there, but I held aloof from them, as I have done all term.

19 DEC. 1863

At 5 went over to the Deanery, where I staid till 8, making a sort of dinner at their tea. The nominal object of my going was to play croquêt, but it never came to that, music, talk, etc. occupying the whole of a _very_ pleasant evening. The Dean was away: Mrs. Liddell was with us part of the time. It is nearly six months (June 25th) since I have seen anything of them, to speak of. I mark this day with a white stone.

12 MAY 1864

During these last few days I have applied in vain for leave to take the children on the river i.e. Alice, Edith, and Rhoda: but Mrs. Liddell will not let _any_ come in the future — rather superfluous caution.

27 MAY 1865

Went with Harcourt by river to Nuneham, taking the eldest three Brodies. We started about 2, and had tea at the house there meeting Miss Harcourt (his cousin) and one of the Misses Hawkins. We got back just in time to witness the races from a little below the Cherwell. Lily rowed a little of the distance.

NUNEHAM

Nuneham, some six miles downstream from Oxford, was a favourite destination for picnic parties during the nineteenth century, thanks to the public-spirited attitude of the owners, the Harcourt family. Their residence, Harcourt House, overlooked grounds which owed much to Lancelot 'Capability' Brown's genius for landscaping, and ran all the way down to the Thames.

Trips down the river to Nuneham feature in many works of Oxford fiction. Tom Brown's future wife made a visit during Commemoration, for instance, and Verdant Green accompanied his own future wife there a decade or so later,

> when in a House-boat and in four-oars, they made ... a wine and water party ... to Nuneham, and, after safely passing through the perils of the pound-locks of Iffley and Sandford, arrived at the pretty thatched cottage, and picknicked in the round-house, and strolled through the nut plantations up to Carfax hill, to see the glorious view of Oxford, ... and paced over the little rustic bridge to the island.

Another author to fall under Nuneham's spell was the American Henry James, who incorporated 'the slanting woods of Nuneham – the sweetest, flattest, reediest, landscape that the heart need demand' into his short story *A Passionate Pilgrim* (1875). En route from Oxford, where they hired a rowing boat near Christ Church Meadow, the two protagonists 'encountered in hundreds the mighty lads of England, clad in white flannel and blue, immense, fair-haired, magnificent in their youth, lounging down the stream in their idle punts, in friendly couples or in solitude or pulling in straining crews and hoarsely exhorted from the bank'.*

Mr and Mrs Hall, in *The Book of the Thames* (1859), observed of Nuneham: 'While Nature has been lavish of her bounties, Art has been employed everywhere to give them due effect. Open glades, solitary walks, graceful slopes, a spacious park, fruitful gardens – in short, all that can attract and charm in English scenery is here gathered.' The estate contained a large wood too, where cottages had been erected for the use of picnickers.

> These pretty and graceful cottages ... exist for the comfort and convenience of pleasure-seekers. Nuneham Courtenay has long been a famous resort of Oxford students and Oxford citizens; and seldom does a summer-day go by without a pleasant 'pic-nic' upon one of its slopes, amid its umbrageous woods, or within the graceful domicile, erected ... for 'public accommodation'.

Alice recalled in 1932 (*Cornhill Magazine*):

> One of our favourite whole-day excursions was to row down to Nuneham, and picnic in the woods there, in one of the huts specially provided by Mr. Harcourt for picknickers. On landing at Nuneham, our first duty was to choose the hut, and then to borrow plates, glasses, knives and forks from the cottages by the riverside. To us the hut might have been a Fairy King's palace, and the picnic a banquet in our honour. Sometimes we were told stories after luncheon that transported us into Fairyland. Sometimes we spent the afternoon wandering in the more material fairyland of the Nuneham woods until it was time to row back to Oxford in the long summer evening.

---

* Repeated almost word for word from a letter James wrote to his brother William from Oxford on 26 April 1869, in which he also alludes to the 'godlike strength' of the competitive rowers.

Occasionally, though, they did not row back, but returned by train. An excursion to Nuneham on 25 June 1863 was a case in point. It was a day almost as important in terms of the creation of 'Alice' as the inception day of 4 July 1862, because it turned out to be last time Carroll ever took the girls out on the river, as far as can be told. But the day was remarkable for other reasons too.

Firstly, it was an altogether unprecedented ensemble: four Liddell sisters this time, as Rhoda, a week before her seventh birthday, came too, with the Dean and Mrs Liddell, and his father, Henry George Liddell (1788–1872). The rowing was undertaken by Carroll, Augustus Harcourt,* and Lord Newry,† making a total of ten, travelling in two boats.

On the journey down to Nuneham, it seems highly likely that the Great Volunteer Review would have been the main topic of conversation. Most if not all of the party had watched it on Port Meadow the day before. The girls' games that day, as they went 'wandering in the more material fairyland of the Nuneham woods', might easily have had a military flavour. And as this is a wooded landscape that Carroll and the Liddell girls all knew well, it is not too fanciful to imagine Nuneham as the transposed setting for the different battle scenes in *Looking-Glass*, where Alice's encounters with Tweedledum and Tweedledee, the White King's soldiers, and the Red and White Knights are all set in or near woods. Manoeuvres of this kind did also take place at Nuneham itself, however. Thomas Plowman, in *In the Days of Victoria* (1918), referred to a 'sham-fight' here when he and William Harcourt (younger brother of Edward) were Volunteers in the early 1860s.

---

* Augustus Harcourt was the nephew of William Vernon Harcourt (1789–1871), then Lord of the Manor of Nuneham. Edith Liddell became engaged to Aubrey Harcourt (1852–1904), the heir, on 13 June 1876, but died suddenly within two weeks of the announcement. She is buried at Christ Church, and there is a stained-glass window to her memory in the Cathedral, by the Pre-Raphaelite artist Edward Burne-Jones.

  More about the history of the Harcourt family appears in *The Abingdon Waterturnpike Murder*, based on a real murder committed on the edge of the Nuneham estate in 1787. In it the River Thames and its bargemen play prominent roles (see page 130).

† Francis Charles Needham (1842–1915).

28. 'Cottages at Nuneham Courtenay' from Mr & Mrs S. C. Hall's *The Book of the Thames* (1859). The rustic cottage and bridge were built specifically to enhance the romantic scene, near the landing place for picnic parties.

The other unprecedented aspect of Thursday 25 June 1863 was that Carroll was permitted to travel back alone with the three older Liddell girls. A fortnight earlier, he had applied a 'white stone' rating to 9 June, when the four of them had also taken a train home (from Abingdon Road Station), also after boating down to Nuneham. But on that occasion Miss Prickett had been present too. This time, Carroll was their sole chaperon, a circumstance which he described as '*mirabile dictu!*' – presumably on account of Ina's presence. She was now 14, and rather too old by the standards of Victorian convention to be unsupervised in the company of a man in his thirties.

One of the abiding mysteries of the relationship between Alice Liddell and Lewis Carroll is why, after this evidently highly satisfactory day of Thursday 25 June 1863, the next page in Carroll's diary is missing, removed after his death, on the grounds presumably that the information there was thought too personal for publication.*

However, a scrap of paper discovered among the Dodgson family papers gives the gist of what the missing page contained. This note, in the handwriting of one of Carroll's nieces, was headed 'Cut pages in Diary', and summarised the contents merely as: Lewis Carroll 'learns from Mrs Liddell that he is supposed to be using the children as a means of paying court to the governess. He is also supposed [by some?] to be courting Ina' (Leach, 1999). In fact, the rumour about Carroll's supposed designs on Miss Prickett had been circulating for years – Carroll had expressed his dismay on the subject as long ago as 1857 – but rumours about Ina would have had far more serious implications, in terms of her reputation and marriage stakes. Probably by mutual consent, therefore, Carroll agreed to keep his distance. No further outings were recorded with any of the Liddells, and even within the confines of Christ Church he remained deliberately 'aloof' for the rest of that year. There was one other encounter away from prying eyes, however, on 19 December 1863, and as Carroll marked this day with a 'white stone', the separation was presumably one he found very hard to take. The next summer, even his offer to take the younger children out was turned down by Mrs Liddell, and the river's appeal seems to have diminished markedly for him as a result. Carroll's diary records only one further trip comparable to the

---

* Carroll did not write a diary entry for every day. Friday 26 June was left blank, but the conclusion to the entry for Saturday 27 June is missing, and possibly the whole of Sunday and Monday too, as Carroll's next complete entry is for Tuesday 30th.

many he had enjoyed in the company of the Liddells, when he took three of the Brodie children to Nuneham in May 1865.*

Carroll must have been much affected by the abrupt end to the 'long dreamy summer afternoons of ancient times', as he described them in a letter to Alice of 21 December 1883 (*Life & Letters*). Memories of this, the last day on which he took any of the Liddell girls out on the river, must surely have coloured Carroll's writing of *Looking-Glass*. Certainly there is particular pathos towards the end, when Carroll's probable alter-ego, the White Knight, says, 'I'll see you safe to the end of the wood – and then I must go back, you know. That's the end of my move.'

It was too. The spoken stories which had had their printed genesis at Godstow, at the upper range of the river trips taken by Carroll and the Liddells, concluded for ever at the downstream extremity of Nuneham. Carroll's imagination was not inhibited, but there were to be no more 'golden afternoons' on the river in the company of the Liddell sisters, no more 'voices and laughter like music over the water' with his favourite 'merry crew', and, sadly for the world of children's literature, no more opportunities for the impromptu creation of further 'news of fairy-land'.

---

* It reflects well on the Harcourts that the delights of Nuneham were open to all. The working-class children of Jericho enjoyed an annual boating treat here in the 1870s, for instance, at the instigation of Thomas and Martha Combe. A former pupil recalled: 'The drum and fife band escorted them to Folly Bridge. At Sandford Lock, a pause for a bun and ginger beer! While on the lawn at Nuneham there was a good tea.' (Davies & Robinson, 2003) Almost certainly, the boat would have been provided by Salters'.

14

'THE END OF MY MOVE'

There are very few further references to the Liddells in Carroll's diaries after that fateful outing to Nuneham in June 1863. Who was holding 'aloof' from whom? It was another seven years before their next really meaningful encounter, which was clearly totally unexpected. Carroll had already been gratified by an opportunity to photograph the University Chancellor's children on 25 June 1870, when 'an almost equally wonderful thing' occurred: 'Mrs Liddell brought Ina and Alice to be photographed ... first visiting my rooms then the studio.'

It seems clear that, without the company of the Liddell girls, rowing became much less of a pleasure for Carroll. He admitted as much to Alice herself, in a letter written on 1 March 1885, when asking her permission to reproduce the original manuscript of 'Alice's Adventures under Ground'. He addressed her formally, as Mrs Hargreaves, and observed that even if his contact seemed 'almost like a voice from the dead, after so many years of silence ... my mental picture is as vivid as ever of one who was, through so many years, my ideal child-friend' (*Life & Letters*).

There are slightly different endings to *Wonderland* and *Under Ground*. In both, Alice awakes on her sister's lap, when the cards fly at her during the trial of the Knave of Hearts. In both versions the cards prove to be leaves, which wake her from her dream, and both texts conclude with the thoughts of this older sister (therefore Ina). Of the two endings, that of *Under Ground* captures the 'Waterland' theme so aptly that I can see no better way to conclude than with the pleasing verisimilitude of Lewis Carroll himself. His penultimate paragraph relates how Alice's sister

> saw an ancient city, and a quiet river winding near it along the plain, and up the stream went slowly gliding a boat with a merry party of children aboard – she could hear their voices and laughter like music over the water – and among them was another little Alice, who sat listening with bright eager eyes to a tale that was being told, and she listened for the words of the tale, and lo! it was the dream of her own little sister. So the boat wound slowly along, beneath the bright summer-day, with its merry crew and its music of voices and laughter, till it passed round one of the many turnings of the stream, and she saw it no more.

APPENDICES

APPENDIX 1

PRICKETT FAMILIES OF BINSEY AND THAME

There can be little doubt that it was Alice Liddell's governess, Mary Prickett (1832–1920), whom Lewis Carroll had largely in mind as the model for the Red Queen – 'the concentrated essence of all governesses' – in *Through the Looking-Glass*. From this deduction, a common assumption arose that, due to the long-established occurrence of the name Prickett in Binsey, Mary must have come from the village. By extension, even though the *Wonderland* treacle well of the Mad Tea-Party is not even in the same book as the Red Queen, it has often been assumed that Mary was also Carroll's source for the story of the well.

There is absolutely no evidence for this, nor can it even be said with certainty that Alice ever visited the well – although it does seem probable, if only because of the connection with her father's college of Christ Church, which held the manorial lordship of Binsey, and was patron of the living (i.e. appointed and paid for curates such as Thomas Prout).

The fact is that Mary Prickett's ancestors came from Thame, an Oxfordshire market town about 12 miles to the east of Oxford. Nonetheless, it is quite possible that some distant family tie did exist between the Pricketts of Binsey and those of Thame, and the short account which follows may prove helpful to further investigation.

There have been Pricketts in Binsey since at least the sixteenth century. The earliest reference in the archives of Christ Church is a document of 1598 (MS Estates 61/107), in which Robert Pricket is named as one of four Binsey yeomen asserting their right to keep cattle on Port Meadow. The implication of this document, maintaining that this right had been applied 'since time out of mind', is that Robert Pricket's ancestors had also lived in the village.

As farmers, the Pricketts continued to be associated with Binsey until the middle of the twentieth century, when Althea Prickett (1880–1973), the last of the family to reside in the village, moved out of the farmhouse, which is the only other building in the immediate vicinity of St Margaret's Church. However, some early members of the Prickett family assumed a more distinctive role: that of the village publican.

Records held at the Oxfordshire Record Office (QSC/A5/1) show that the earliest identifiable licence for a Binsey alehouse was dated April 1651. This was issued in the name of Thomas Prickett, who remained licensed until 1661, followed by other members of the Prickett family – Alice, John, and (presumably) another Thomas – until the early eighteenth century. Binsey was near one of the principal fords across the Thames into Oxford from the west, and its public house must therefore have benefited from passing trade, both on land and on water. In earlier times, the proximity of the famous well of St Frideswide seems certain to have engendered additional custom too, especially as the path through Binsey linked two other important religious communities: Godstow Nunnery to the north and the enormous abbey at Osney (until it was dismantled in the sixteenth century) to the south. There are accounts (almost certainly exaggerated, but presumed to have some basis in fact) that the neighbouring, now-vanished, village of Seacourt boasted in the medieval period some two dozen inns and lodging houses specifically to cater for visitors to the well.

The only tenuous connection to link the Pricketts of Binsey with those of Thame comes from the journal (*Remarks and Collections*, Oxford Historical Society, 1902 & 1914) of Thomas Hearne (1678–1735), the Oxford antiquary and Bodleian librarian. Hearne visited Binsey on 22 December 1718, noting 'an old well on the West Side of Binsey Church which they call St. Margaret's Well. They say it hath been very famous.' On the same day he spoke to Thomas Prickett, perhaps the second publican of this name above, but who was by then a yeoman farmer. Prickett, who had been born about 1658, and his wife had then one daughter living at home, one married and living at Iffley, and a married son living in Binsey. Thomas Prickett had been a church warden at Binsey for 38 years.

When the two men met again in 1728, Prickett told Hearne that as a member of the Militia he had provided military instruction at Thame School at the time of Monmouth's Rebellion (of 1685). Is it possible that Thame was a deliberate choice, on account of his having relatives in the town? The first appearance of the name Prickett in the records of St Mary's Church at Thame comes a few years later, when John Prickett, the son of John, was baptised on 19 December 1692. From him, the line to Mary Prickett was as follows: Thomas, son of John, baptised 27 May 1703; Giles, son of Thomas, baptised 11 April 1734; Loder, son of Giles, baptised 22 February 1766, all in Thame.

The occupations of the earlier Pricketts of Thame are unknown, but Giles was an attorney, a profession also followed by his son, Loder, who married Martha Langford in Oxford in 1790. Their son James, Mary Prickett's father, was baptised at St Michael at the Northgate in Oxford on 27 January 1793. James married in 1826, and Mary was his third child, baptised at St Clement's in Oxford on 29 January 1832, when James described himself as a 'gentleman', living in Cowley Road. By the time of the 1841 Census, James Prickett was living with his 85-year-old mother, Martha, a woman of independent means, in one of the grand terraced townhouses of Beaumont Street in central Oxford, with his wife Elizabeth and family of six children, aged between two and thirteen years, and three servants. At the time he called himself a 'college servant', and he remained in this employment all his life, specifically as a butler of Trinity College in 1847 (*Post Office Directory*) and 1861, by which time the family was living in the very much more modest surroundings of Floyd's Row, a few minutes' walk from Christ Church.

Mary Prickett found employment with the Liddells very soon after they came to Oxford, and is first mentioned in Carroll's diaries on 3 November 1856. She left their service to marry, at the age of 40, a wealthy wine merchant, a widower called Charles Foster (1809–1888). The ceremony was held at St Aldate's Church, immediately opposite Christ Church, on 22 March 1871. Her father, somewhat presumptuously, persisted in describing himself as a 'gentleman'.

This was not the first Foster–Prickett union. In an intriguing cross-generational alliance, Mary's younger sister Elizabeth (1837–1914) had married Charles Foster's son, John (1838–1873), in 1864. Then their brother Frederick Prickett (1842–?) married Charles Foster's daughter Anne (1841–?) in 1873! On the death of her husband that same year, Elizabeth married Samuel Patey Spiers (1840–?), son of Richard James Spiers (1806–1877), whose diary is featured on page 113. Once married, Charles and Mary Foster took over Oxford's most prestigious coaching inn, The Mitre, in the High Street. It was to be Mary's home for the rest of her life. Caryl Hargreaves remembered (*Cornhill Magazine*, July 1932):

> On one occasion when Oxford was very full, my grandfather [Henry Liddell] persuaded Mrs Foster to turn out of her own rooms in the hotel in order to provide accommodation for Lord Rosebury. The latter, who knew all the Liddell family well, said to the Dean that he was surprised to find the rooms of the proprietress of the Mitre Hotel full of photographs of the Liddells, and wondered how she had got them!

Surviving her husband by more than 30 years, Mary Foster continued to run The Mitre (residing with her sister, brother-in-law, and

29. (LEFT) Miss Prickett, a photograph of unknown date and origin *(courtesy of Hodder & Stoughton)*.
30. (RIGHT) Tenniel's Red Queen and Alice in 'The Garden of Live Flowers'.

numerous nephews and nieces) until her death in 1920 – a tenancy of almost half a century!

It would therefore appear that there is no direct connection between Mary Prickett and Binsey – even though it is tempting to discern an ancestral echo, just possibly, of those early Binsey publicans in her later occupation. Indeed, her father had also been a 'wine merchant' in the early years of his marriage. It is by no means impossible that there was some connection. A hundred years later the Rev. Arnold Mallinson was in no doubt. In a parish newsletter of February 1967 (reprinted in *Quinquagesimo*, 1974) he stated confidently that Mary Prickett had been the great aunt of a Miss Prickett then resident in the village. He did not name her, but it is clear that he was referring to Althea Prickett (who always maintained that her family's presence in Binsey went back to Saxon times), about whom – and about Binsey in general – more appears in *A Towpath Walk in Oxford* (see page 129).

APPENDIX 2

TRILL MILL STREAM

An interesting reference is made to the Trill Mill Stream and 'Alice's Shop' in J. C. Masterman's novel *To Teach the Senators Wisdom*. The book consists largely of the deliberations of a group of Oxford dons who are trying to decide which of the city's many highlights they should show to some American visitors. One of the more unorthodox suggestions is 'the authentic sweet shop which Alice visited in *Through the Looking-glass*'. Masterman's book was published in 1952, when post-World War Two shortages were still apparent in the proponent's rationale for his choice:

> It seems to me that in that shop the Oxford of Lewis Carroll is still alive. Sweet ration or no sweet ration, I dare swear that the sweets in those glass bottles have not been changed since Tenniel drew them. I sometimes think that that odd world was the real Oxford. Is there any historical Oxford character better known than the White Knight or even the Walrus and the Carpenter?

Another of the dons is reminded of an Oxford undergraduate tradition, that of negotiating the underground section of the Trill Mill Stream in a punt or canoe, saying:

> I fancy, though I don't know for certain, that this particular drain or waterway is used by Carroll when Alice makes her journey with the sheep. I made the journey myself one summer afternoon with three other men, and it so happened that when we emerged in what was then the new Christ Church Memorial Garden some people were leaning over the stone balustrade and looking at the stream as it flowed lazily out of the ground. Their faces when our canoe emerged stick in my memory – you see, it happened to be the day of Encaenia* and two of

---

* The ceremonial conferring of degrees as part of Commemoration.

us were in morning coats and top-hats. I think that scene would have pleased Lewis Carroll; certainly we must have looked not unlike a Mad Hatter's water picnic.

The pioneer of these subterranean journeys seems to have been T. E. Lawrence (1888–1935), better known as 'Lawrence of Arabia'. Lawrence came to Oxford with his parents in 1896, living in a house very close to the Oxford Canal, and studied at Jesus College from 1907 to 1910. There are several accounts by friends who accompanied Lawrence on these underground adventures, the first probably being in 1908. It was described as 'no mad cap adventure. On the contrary, it was planned in every detail' (*T. E. Lawrence by his Friends*, ed. A. W. Lawrence, 1937). Among the plans was Lawrence's intention to shock his fellow explorers, and indeed the whole neighbourhood, 'for he had concealed in his pocket a .450 revolver and blank cartridges, and these he fired off without warning in the narrow pitch-dark tunnel' (*Jesus College Magazine*, June 1935).

Some years later, the locality near the Trill Mill Stream exit underwent lasting change. R. T. Gunther of Magdalen College wrote to *Notes & Queries* (21 February 1925) to note that the 'pulling down of high houses over the way has let light into that "little dark shop" ... the only shop in St. Aldates that has retained its original small-paned windows and the counter as shown in the pictures [of Tenniel]'. He went on to say: 'The bottles with sweets are there, but trade in toys has gone a few doors down the street, the "AꟼT" at 2s has become a brand of chocolate, and the dolls are replaced by bananas.'

Given the modern dominance of national supermarket chains, the conclusion to Gunther's letter reads with great poignancy: 'It is but a tiny shop, where humble folk can live for a small rent and make an honest livelihood. More such are wanted. May the day be far distant when Oxford, wholly in the grasp of the multi-store keeper, cannot stimulate the imagination of her Lewis Carrolls, and their juvenile readers.'

APPENDIX 3
HATTER MATTER

Lewis Carroll always denied that any of his characters were based on real people; his illustrator John Tenniel always denied caricaturing a real face. Whether or not this was true, few subsequent commentators have wanted to believe it. Certainly it seems logical that Carroll might create characters and scenes that Alice would recognise. Yet if that was the case, the common assertion that the Hatter was based on an Oxford furniture maker called Theophilus Carter seems immediately suspect, as there is no evidence whatsoever of any acquaintanceship. Thomas Randall, on the other hand, certainly was known to Alice, and was also an actual hatter, which, in any comparison, gives him immediately what might be termed a head start!

However, before presenting Randall's credentials, the case for Theophilus Carter warrants analysis, if only because it appears never to have been seriously questioned. And in so doing, the unanswerable nature of this particular Carrollian puzzle becomes apparent, through a chance association which leads from Carter to a third candidate, Francis T. Cooper. Whatever the truth of the matter, a brief account of these three prominent Oxford tradesmen can only be helpful in setting the contemporary Oxford scene.

Theophilus Carter (*c*1824–1904)
On 7 March 1931, *The Times* listed some memorable items from the 1851 Great Exhibition at Crystal Palace. Among them was an 'alarm clock bed which tipped the occupant out at the appointed hour'. This prompted Mr W. J. Ryland to comment (10 March) that the bed had been Theophilus Carter's invention. In response, Mr W. H.

Greene (13 March) pointed out that Carter's still greater claim to fame was as 'the doubtless unconscious model for the Mad Hatter', adding that 'the likeness was unmistakable'. A third correspondent, Rev. W. Gordon Baillie, endorsed this idea (19 March), writing that

> all Oxford called him 'The Mad Hatter' and ... he would stand at the door of his furniture shop in the High, sometimes in an apron, always with a top-hat at the back of his head, which, with a well-developed nose and a somewhat receding chin, made him an easy target for the caricaturist.

Baillie added that 'the story went' that Carroll, 'thinking T. C. had imposed on him, took this revenge'. The correspondence concluded (20 March 1931) with a second letter from Ryland. Although he had known Carter reasonably well, he had been unaware of this Carrollian association (so evidently 'all Oxford' did *not* know!), but concurred that Tenniel's Hatter was 'he to the life'.

On the face of it, these three opinions, albeit expressed so very retrospectively, seem fairly persuasive, and the 'Theo Theory' has over time become accepted by many as fact. Yet closer investigation refutes Mr Ryland's initial claim about Carter. Certainly, an 'alarum bedstead'* was exhibited at the 1851 Great Exhibition – in fact two were – but neither is attributed to Carter in the *Official Descriptive and Illustrated Catalogue* (the title page of which, coincidentally, earned John Tenniel his first important acclaim).

Further doubt derives from the memories of the lifelong Oxford resident Thomas F. Plowman (*In the Days of Victoria*, 1918), who was taken to the Exhibition as a seven-year-old. The 'bed that turned people out if they did not get up in time' was one of the three things that he most wanted to see. Yet he makes no reference to its having Oxford origins, even though his own father had been 'secretary

---

* A similar, though less ambitious, device features in *Verdant Green*.

of the Exhibition' for Oxfordshire and 'an exhibitor of one or two inventions' himself. One of the two beds was exhibited by Robert Watson Savage, the other by Theodore Jones. Theodore? Theophilus? Did someone, at some point, get confused, perhaps? And if that key claim of *The Times'* correspondents is incorrect, one wonders how much faith to place in their other pronouncements ...

The *facts* of Theophilus Carter's life are that he was christened at St Aldate's Church, opposite Christ Church, on 1 June 1824, the son of Harriet and Thomas Carter, a 'college servant'. He married Mary Ann Clarkson (*c*1822–1887) at Wolvercote on 13 April 1846, at which time his father was described as a cook.

By 1851, the year of the Great Exhibition, Theophilus and Mary, now with three children, were living just off Oxford's High Street. He is described as a 'porter/cabinet maker'. For the rest of his working life (from at least 1861 until 1894), Carter lived and worked at 49 High Street, and occupied No. 48 in addition between 1875 and 1883.*

Carter was buried at St Peter-in-the-East on Christmas Eve 1904, aged 80. He had been one of two overseers for the parish in 1865 and 1894 (and presumably other years too). In the latter year he shared the role with Frank Cooper (1844–1927), who produced his (wife's) famous Oxford marmalade on the opposite side of the street from about 1874 until 1900.

Francis T. Cooper (1811–1862)

In the context of this appendix, the name Cooper proves to be of more than simply passing interest. Why? Well, because a particular aspect of the career of Frank Cooper's father, Francis Thomas Cooper, encourages his inclusion as a third possible influence for Carroll's Hatter.

---

* The premises at No. 48, meanwhile, have a later connection with a truly iconic Oxford name. William Morris (1834–1896), prior to his great motor-car enterprises, repaired and manufactured cycles and motor bicycles here from 1896 to 1908.

The Hatter is both described and depicted as wearing a hat and having a predilection for tea. There is nothing especially strange in that. What might be considered strange, however, is a shop *selling* both hats and tea, which is exactly what Francis T. Cooper had. He was trading as a hatter at 46 High Street by 1839 (*Robson's Directory*) and was still listed as such in 1846 (*Hunt's Directory*). A hatter was also how he described himself in the 1841 Census. Yet in 1845 he had placed an advert in *Jackson's Oxford Journal* (18 October 1845) which showed that he had also been an agent for Ridgway's Teas for nearly six years: a somewhat eccentric – might one say 'mad'?! – combination.* Whether he was still doing so by the time Carroll arrived in Oxford, in 1851, is not known.

Thomas Randall (1805–1887)

Thomas Randall was born on 5 September 1805, the son of a mercer. He was well educated at New College School, but nonetheless destined for a career in the family business, and in 1827 married his cousin, the eldest daughter of his deceased uncle, Josiah Randall, a hatter in Cornmarket Street. She died within two years of marriage, and he was remarried in 1830, to Elizabeth Cecil, the daughter of a solicitor. By 1835 Randall was trading as a hatter in his own right (*Vincent's Directory*) at the premises that he would occupy all his working life at 22 High Street.

Many are the accounts, both in memoirs and fiction, of Oxford students running up enormous bills on tick, both parties being confident that the arrears would eventually be settled through parental intervention. Sometimes that confidence was misplaced, and Randall found himself at the forefront of a notorious bankruptcy trial in 1847.

---

* In 1856 he moved across the High to the larger premises at No. 84 from which the Cooper name would become world-famous. Interested readers will find more in *Cooper's Oxford* by Brigid Allen (1989).

When the case against a Worcester College undergraduate called Edward Napleton Jennings was discharged, 64 Oxford tradesmen were left out-of-pocket.* One of them was Thomas Randall, 'Hatter', whose premises had been specifically singled out as a 'ruination' shop. The magistrate had decided that it was not reasonable to expect an ingenuous young man to resist 'every species of credit proffered for every species of extravagance', prompting *The Times* to hope that its readers would 'heartily rejoice' at the verdict, believing that Oxford's 'trade harpies' (or 'honey-tongued bloodsuckers', in the words of one correspondent) had got what they deserved. This prompted Randall to publish a pamphlet, *Oxford tradesmen versus the insolvent Jennings*, in defence of the much maligned shopkeepers.

Standing up for Oxford's 'shopocracy' evidently did Randall no harm. In *Oxford Memories* (1886), James Pycroft, a Trinity College don, described him as the 'link between the town and the gown'. One unorthodox such 'link' was a service that surely few of his peers could match: G. W. Kitchin (who went for occasional rows on the river with Lewis Carroll) recalled that Randall, 'the great hosier of the High', would 'for a consideration' compose weekly essays for undergraduates to present as their own work (*Ruskin in Oxford*, 1904). Pycroft too remembered that Randall 'was scholar enough to do verses and essays, as well as impositions, for the incapable and the idle'. By the 1850s his fame was sufficient to warrant inclusion in the humorous novel *The Adventures of Mr. Verdant Green*. Among the debts which Green, conforming to type, accrues as an

31. Alderman Thomas Randall (1805–1887), post-1861.

---

* Francis Cooper was not among them: his 1845 advertisement specified 'for ready money only, the small profit obtained admitting of neither credit nor risk'.

32. (LEFT) Tenniel's Hatter and Dormouse at the Mad Tea-Party.
33. (RIGHT) Thomas Randall, date unknown (*courtesy of David Pennant*).

undergraduate is one with Randall for the Oxford-blue tie that he later wears at his wedding.

In the 1841 and 1851 Censuses, Randall called himself a 'hatter and hosier', and in 1861, 'magistrate and hatter'. By this time he was living in Grandpont House, near Folly Bridge, a location of which Alice had a lasting memory (see page 54). Grandpont House was built in 1785 for Oxford's then Town Clerk, Elias Taunton. The three-storey building overlooked the stretch of the River Thames where the college rowing races finished. This was an activity in which Randall took an active interest. William Tuckwell (*Reminiscences*, 1907) remembered how the eight-oar boat used in a famous race against Cambridge in 1843 (see Appendix 5) had stood 'rotten and decayed' opposite Grandpont House, where the Trill Mill Stream joins the Thames. In 1867, the boat 'was bought by jolly Tom Randall, mercer, alderman, scholar, its sound parts fashioned into a chair, and presented as the President's throne to the University barge' (see Appendix 4). This surprising gesture by a non-University man is another endorsement of Randall's credentials as a Town and Gown 'link'.

Quite how often Alice visited Grandpont House we shall never know. But there are some clues in the diary of Randall's only daughter, Elizabeth (1836–1916), and I am grateful to John Stainer, a descendant, for providing the following sample entries. Towards the end of 1862, the Liddells' governess Mary Prickett (whom Elizabeth called Polly) was a frequent visitor, often in the company of her 'chicks' (as Elizabeth dubbed the Liddell girls). The walks that she (and Rover, the Randalls' retriever, presumably!) took with them all on 24 November and on 8 & 15 December 1862 were unremarkable, but on 12 December she recorded: '*Polly and the children came down and we went to Iffley and home by road. Alice L's side bad*'. Then on 22 December '*Polly called with Alice and Edith. Joe and I went with them to Bagley Wood*'. It was only the two 'chicks' on this occasion, because '*Ina at Cheltenham with Mrs L.*'.*

A second unpublished diary, that of Richard James Spiers (1806–1877), another respected High Street shopkeeper (also featured in *Verdant Green*), shows that Mary Prickett (whom the Spiers also knew as 'Polly') was moving in the same social circles as the Randalls towards the end of her period of service with the Liddells. Spiers records her attendance at two dinner parties, on 21 January 1867 and 7 January 1868, at which Mr & Mrs Randall and Dr & Mrs Stainer (parents of John Stainer, 1840–1901, who married Elizabeth Randall in 1865) were also present.† John Stainer, later knighted for services to music, introduces another strong Christ Church association, as he graduated there, and, according to Anne Clark in *The Real Alice*, was

---

* The girls' grandparents on their father's side lived in Cheltenham.
† Two other pertinent entries from Spiers' diary (all published here for the first time, with thanks to the Oxford Architectural & Historical Society) are that he and some friends called on Charles Dodgson on 16 February 1862. He also dined with him in his rooms on 7 June 1862: '*Pleasant evening*' was Spiers' verdict; '*very pleasant evening*' was Carroll's!

34. A (slightly cropped) photograph (estimated at 1864/65) including, as identified by John Stainer: in the middle row Sir James Morrish (grey hat), sometime Mayor of London, and Thomas Randall (black top hat); and at the back Eliza (Mrs Thomas) Randall in the centre and her daughter Elizabeth Cecil Randall (later Lady Stainer) to the right. The other people in the picture are from the Margetson family, who were close friends of the Randalls. *(Photo courtesy of David Pennant)*

often invited to the Deanery because 'Alice loved music, too, and the Liddells did a great deal to encourage music in Oxford'.

Randall, who served as a town councillor from 1833, was elected Mayor in 1859, and became an Alderman in 1861, retired from business in 1864, after which, if the 1881 Census entry is any guide, he thought of himself as a 'retired hatter'. When he died in 1887, the enduring Christ Church association is clear from the presence of the Dean's carriage at the funeral. His obituary in *Jackson's* of 24 September 1887 emphasised his generosity to the poorer children of the parish, and provided another example of his combined Town and Gown status as the instigator of a scheme to provide summer vacation employment at seaside resorts for otherwise redundant (and therefore unpaid) college servants.

Tenniel's Hatter

Even though John Tenniel (1820–1914) was already very well known as the chief illustrator of *Punch* in the 1860s, he was not above basing many of his *Wonderland* images on ideas that the unknown Carroll had originally drawn for Alice in 'Under Ground'. The Hatter did not appear there, however, the character having been introduced later. So the inspiration for the Hatter's visual appearance seems to be solely down to Tenniel. There is no firm evidence that Tenniel came to Oxford at the relevant time, to enable him to observe likely local residents.

One opportunity might have been in the early summer of 1865, as (according to Rodney Engen in *Alice's White Knight*) that is when he had taken 'his annual river row' on the Oxfordshire Thames, visiting Nuneham 'and those nearby areas familiar to Dodgson'. Another visit is alluded to by Tenniel himself, in some verses he composed under the title 'From Oxford to Henley'. In *Artist of Wonderland*, Frankie Morris places this trip as approximately 1871. Certainly, the fact that this annual rowing holiday started at Salters' yard would have given Tenniel every chance to visit the supposed Sheep's shop (see page 40) in St Aldate's, just a few minutes' walk away. With his photographic memory, Tenniel would have needed only one look.*

But to return to the Hatter. In 'The Lion and the Unicorn', Tenniel's familiar participant at the 'Mad Tea-Party' and witness in 'Who Stole the Tarts?' has become the White King's Messenger, called Hatta (still drinking tea!). He is accompanied by the Anglo-

---

* One other visit by Tenniel occurred after *Looking-Glass* had already been printed. Richard Spiers' diary entries for 12 & 13 July 1872 show that he spent most of the day with what he called the 'Punch party', which included Tenniel. He spent both days 'lionizing' with them, joined them for dinner at the Randolph Hotel, and entertained them at his home.

Saxon Messenger,* Haigha, pronounced 'to rhyme with "mayor" ', in other words that second émigré from *Wonderland*, the erstwhile March Hare. The King says to Haigha at one point, 'You alarm me', which could be construed as an allusion to Carter's reputed 1851 bed. As indeed might the Hatter's obsession with time and repeated efforts to wake up the sleepy Dormouse at the Tea-Party. The puzzle is compounded by a passing comment in Collingwood's *Life & Letters*, who refers to someone whom no commentator has ever identified: a member of Carroll's dining room 'mess' at Christ Church who was 'one who still lives in "Alice in Wonderland" as the "Hatter"'.

Whatever the reality of the influences on these two supremely creative minds, it is clear that Francis Cooper - known for selling tea with his hats - Thomas Randall – known for selling hats – and Theophilus Carter – reputedly known for wearing one in particular – were, each of them, prominent Oxford characters. Whether any of them also inspired that prominent Wonderland character we shall never truly know.

Of the three, Thomas Randall always thought of himself first and foremost as an actual hatter, a man who might even have said within Carroll's hearing: 'I keep them to sell... I've none of my own. I'm a hatter.' And if it really *was* Randall whom Carroll had in mind, these words from his 1887 obituary in *Jackson's Oxford Journal* are more apt than the writer could possibly have imagined: Randall (or, if you prefer, the Hatter) 'has left a name behind him that will long be affectionately remembered not only in the homes of the rich, but in the cottage homes of the poor'.

---

* I cannot resist mentioning the Messenger's 'Anglo-Saxon attitudes', a phrase adopted as the title of the 1956 novel by my great-uncle Angus Wilson. The book's theme of academic rivalry and fraud may (or may not!) have been influenced by his experiences as an Oxford undergraduate of the 1930s.

APPENDIX 4

OXFORD COLLEGE BARGES

During the 1860s and 1870s the status of rowing and rowers within the University went from strength to strength, and the importance of the college barges – threefold in purpose: as changing and storage rooms, as viewing platforms, and as college status symbols – increased accordingly. The records of the various college boat clubs are often incomplete, but from Clare Sheriff's *The Oxford College Barges* (2003, from which most of the following information derives) it would seem that some ten or twelve barges, including some which were rented from Salter Brothers, would have graced the bank of Christ Church Meadow during Alice's childhood.

The first of these grandiose vessels ever to be seen in Oxford was a former London livery company barge, used by the Merchant Taylors for ceremonial occasions. It was purchased by the Oxford University Boat Club in 1846, three years after the famous Oxford–Cambridge race of 1843, which elevated the importance of rowing as a University sport (see Appendix 5). This first barge passed to University College in 1854, to be replaced by a new, purpose-built vessel designed by E. G. Bruton. Bruton's is therefore the vessel referred to in Mr & Mrs S. C. Hall's 1859 *Book of the Thames*; it appeared to them as they passed 'sombre in style', but was subsequently 'richly decorated with colour, and displaying the armorial bearings of all the colleges'.

The export of ceremonial vessels from London to Oxford continued with Oriel College's purchase of what is believed to have been the Goldsmiths' Company barge before 1850. Exeter College (also referred to by the Halls) acquired the Stationers' barge in 1856, and purchased a second from Salter Brothers in 1873. This is an early example of what would become a lucrative business for the firm, which already rented barges to Trinity in 1866 and Magdalen in 1872. Balliol purchased the Skinners' barge in 1859, and Queen's owned the former Lord Mayor of London's barge from about 1860. Other colleges – Brasenose, Christ Church, and Pembroke for certain – also possessed their own barges at this time, Pembroke sharing theirs with New, St John's, and Jesus colleges after 1877.

Today little trace of this unusual fleet remains. Many barges survived until the twentieth century, but by the late 1930s their historical functions started to be fulfilled by permanent boat houses a little farther downstream (see page 63), and most of the barges themselves were broken up or dispersed. However, the former barges of Queen's (1903), Corpus Christi (1930), and St John's (1891) colleges can still be seen in the Oxford area (at Medley, above Iffley, and above Sandford respectively). Until 2011 part of the barge built by Salters for Keble College in 1898 was displayed at the Museum of Oxford in St Aldate's (where various items of Liddell and Carroll memorabilia are on view).

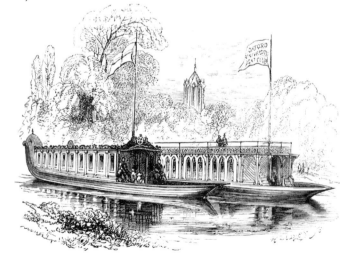

35. 'State Barges' from Mr & Mrs S. C. Hall's *The Book of the Thames* (1859). The two vessels shown are the former Stationers' Company barge, purchased by Exeter College in 1846, and the new University Boat Club barge, built in 1856.

APPENDIX 5

THE OXFORD–CAMBRIDGE BOAT RACE
OF 1843

The Oxford–Cambridge boat race of 1843 is widely acknowledged as the one that changed the status of rowing in Oxford, from a minor pastime to the pre-eminent university sport. In *Reminiscences* (ed. 2, 1907), the Rev. W. Tuckwell called this 1843 race at Henley 'the event which really popularised boating in Oxford; the College races were before that year a mere pleasant incident in a summer term, there were no college barges on the river; even the Oxford and Cambridge race, except in 1829, the first race rowed, excited languid interest'.

The circumstance which made the 1843 race so special was that Oxford triumphed despite being a man down. The all-important position of stroke was filled by an exceptional oarsman called Fletcher Menzies, who had inspired a great improvement in the Oxford performance, after several years of Cambridge victories. Expectations were high. Then, just before the race, Menzies was suddenly taken ill and had to withdraw. As the rules permitted no substitute, the seven men of Oxford, 'hopeless of more than a creditable defeat', as Tuckwell put it, took to their oars. Thomas Hughes' brother George was a member of the crew, and he switched position to row stroke. Despite the odds, Oxford won. Hysterical celebrations followed, as witnessed by Thomas Hughes, who recorded in *Memoir of a Brother* (ed.2, 1873):

The crew had positively to fight their way into their hotel, and barricade themselves there, to escape being carried round Henley on our shoulders. The enthusiasm, frustrated in this direction, burst out in all sorts of follies, of which you may take this as a specimen. The heavy toll-gate was pulled down, and thrown over the bridge into the river, by a mob of young Oxonians headed by a small, decorous, shy man in spectacles, who had probably never pulled an oar in his life.

Tuckwell's account of the post-victory mischief concurred, noting that after gathering at The Red Lion in Henley, the jubilant Oxonians 'tore up a heavy toll-bar gate, and flung it over the bridge into the river'. Neither account condemns the damage, which is rather in keeping with the kind of drunken vandalism regularly attributed – and again with little sense of disapproval – to Oxford undergraduates in many an Oxford novel of the nineteenth century. There is also a long account in volume two of *Memories of Oxford* (1886) by the Oxford don James Pycroft. It was 'as if all Henley were raving mad at once', he wrote.

'One effect the seven-oar race had on our generation at Oxford: it made boating really popular, which it had not been till then,' wrote Thomas Hughes, who himself took up rowing soon after, with instant success (much like the eponymous hero of *Tom Brown at Oxford*): he was in a victorious Oriel College four-oar crew the following year. His brother George was captain, 'and no man ever knew better when to give his crew the long Abingdon reach, and when to be content with Iffley and Sandford. At the half-hour's rest at those places he would generally sit quiet, and watch the skittles, wrestling, quoits, or feats of strength which were going on all about.' Hughes' overall verdict was that 'there are few pleasanter memories of my life than those of the river-side'. His love of the Thames shows in the long and vivid descriptions in *Tom Brown at Oxford,* and his competitive nature shows in the line from the book which justifies all the hard work, on the final day of racing, 'with all Oxford looking on, when the prize is the headship of the river – once in a generation do men get such a chance'.

The Oxford boat used in the famous 1843 victory 'was moored as a trophy in Christchurch meadow at the point where Pactolus poured its foul stream into the Isis', according to Tuckwell, another writer unable to resist the temptation to allude to the disreputable nature of the Trill Mill Stream. By 1867, very little of the boat remained. According to James Pycroft, Thomas Randall (the city alderman whose dog sometimes accompanied Alice Liddell on her walks) 'made a chair of the timbers of the winning boat, and presented it, inscribed with the names of the famous crew, to the University barge' (see Appendix 3).

SOURCES AND FURTHER READING

'BEDE', 'Cuthbert' — *The Adventures of Mr. Verdant Green*, Blackwood, London, Parts 1 to 3, 1853–57 (Rev. Edward Bradley)

CARROLL, Lewis — *Alice's Adventures in Wonderland*, Macmillan, London, 1865

Through the Looking-Glass, Macmillan, London, 1872

Alice's Adventures under Ground, Macmillan, London, 1886

'Alice on the Stage' in *The Theatre,* April 1887

CHURCH, Alfred J. — *Isis and Thamesis*, Seeley & Co, London, 1886

CLARK, Anne — *The Real Alice*, Michael Joseph, London, 1981

COLLINGWOOD, Stuart Dodgson (ed.) — *Life and Letters of Lewis Carroll,* T. Fisher Unwin, London, 1898

The Lewis Carroll Picture Book, T. Fisher Unwin, London, 1899

DAVIES, Mark & ROBINSON, Catherine — *A Towpath Walk in Oxford*, Oxford Towpath Press, 2003

GARDNER, Martin — *The Annotated Alice,* Norton, New York, 2000

GORDON, Colin — *Beyond the Looking Glass,* Hodder & Stoughton, London, 1982

HALL, Mr. & Mrs. S. C. — *The Book of the Thames*, Arthur Hall, Virtue & Co, London, 1859 (first serialised in *The Art-Journal*, 1857–58)

HARGREAVES, Caryl — 'Alice's Recollections of Carrollian Days', *Cornhill Magazine*, July 1932

HIBBERT, C. & E. (eds.) — *Encyclopaedia of Oxford*, Macmillan, London, 1988

HOLMAN-HUNT, William — *Pre-Raphaelitism and the Pre-Raphaelite Brotherhood*, Chapman & Hall, London, 1913 (ed. 2)

HUGHES, Thomas — *Tom Brown at Oxford*, Macmillan, London, 1861 (ed. 3 of 1914)

JEROME, Jerome K. — *Three Men in a Boat*, J. W. Arrowsmith, Bristol, 1889, (Oxford University Press, 1998)

JONES, Jo Elwyn & GLADSTONE, Francis — *The Alice Companion*, New York University Press, 1998

LEACH, Karoline — *In the Shadow of the Dreamchild*, Peter Owen, London, 1999

RIMMER, Alfred — *Pleasant Spots Around Oxford*, Cassell, Potter, & Galpin, London, 1878

RUSKIN, John — *Praeterita*, G. Allen, Orpington, (in parts) 1885–89

SHERRIFF, Clare — *The Oxford College Barges*, Unicorn, London, 2003

TAUNT, Henry — *A New Map of the River Thames*, Taunt, Oxford (ed. 2) 1873 and (ed. 3) 1879

WAKELING, Edward — *Lewis Carroll's Diaries*, (January 1855–April 1858, May 1862–December 1897 in nine volumes), Lewis Carroll Society, 1993–2007

INDEX

References to Christ Church, Lewis Carroll, Alice Liddell, her siblings (Harry, Lorina, and Edith), and her parents have not been included, nor individuals mentioned in passing in Carroll's diaries.

Abingdon 18, 71, 87, 89, 120
Arnold, Matthew 57
Aston's Eyot, Oxford 63

Bagley Wood 53, 113
Barrie, J.M. 82
'Bede, Cuthbert' 42, 55
Beesley family 15, 17, 20
Binsey 15, 20–27, 29, 32, 36, 63,
    100–102, 104
Blenheim Palace 36
Bossom, C. & family 15, 17, 20
Botanical Gardens, Oxford 68
Boughton, Mary 79, 80
Bradley, Edward 42, 49, 55
Brodie, Benjamin & family 52, 61, 90, 96
Brown, Lancelot 'Capability' 91
Bruton, E. G. 117
Buckland, Francis 47
Bulstake Stream 32
Burne-Jones, Edward 93

Cambridge 57, 112, 117, 119
Carter, Theophilus 107–109
Carter, Thomas & Harriet 109
Castle Mill Stream 15
Cecil, Eliza(beth) (later Randall) 110,
    113, 114
Chamberlain, Rev. Thomas 30, 35
Chaucer, Geoffrey 41
Cheltenham 113
Cherwell River 39, 42, 48, 59, 60,
    62–64, 90
Church, Alfred 15
Clarkson, Mary Ann 109
Clifton Hampden 89

Collingwood, Stuart Dodgson 8, 11,
    58, 116
Combe, Thomas & Martha 29–35, 96
Cooper, Francis Thomas 109–111
Cooper, Frank 109
Cowley 75
Culham 89

Darwin, Charles 81
Daudet, Alphonse 25
Davies, Michael Llewellyn 82
Disraeli, Benjamin 36
Dodgson, Rev. Charles ix, 33
Dodgson, Edwin ix, 31, 60, 63
Dodgson, Elizabeth ix, 30, 79–81
Dodgson, Frances ('Fanny') ix, 30, 80,
    81
Dodgson, Mrs Frances Jane ix
Dodgson Skeffington ix, 4, 60
Dodgson Wilfred ix, 60
Duckworth, Robinson 4, 7, 8, 37, 39, 74,
    79–81

Eights' Week 37, 56, 66, 69

Fellows, Mrs Pleasance E. 50, 58
Floyd's Row 39, 48, 103
Folly Bridge, Oxford 37–39, 54, 56, 59, 65,
    69, 112
Foster, Anne 103
Foster, Charles 103
Foster, John 103
Four Streams 32

Gaisford, Thomas & William 82
Godstow x, 3–10, 81, 96, 101

Grahame, Kenneth & Alastair 82
Grandpont House, Oxford 54, 59, 112, 113

Hackman, Rev. Alfred 31
Hall, Mr & Mrs Samuel Carter 24, 55,
    92, 94, 117, 118
Hall, Thomas 37
Harcourt, Aubrey 93
Harcourt, Augustus George Vernon 5, 9,
    52, 89, 90, 93
Harcourt, Edward William 5, 53, 92
Harcourt, William Vernon 93
Hargreaves, Caryl 8, 37, 47, 103
Hargreaves, Reginald xiv
Head of the River pub 37–39
Hearne, Thomas 101, 102
Henley-on-Thames 115, 119, 120
Hinksey villages 53, 61, 63
Holman Hunt, William 31, 35
Hopkins, Gerard Manley 32
Hughes, George 57, 119, 120
Hughes, Thomas 57, 69, 71, 119, 120

Iffley 67–71, 79, 80, 91, 113, 118, 120
Isis Lock, Oxford 32
Isis Tavern, Iffley 67, 69

James, Henry 91, 92
James, William 92
Jennings, Edward Napleton 111
Jericho 29–35, 60, 96
Jerome, Jerome K. 37, 89
Jones, Theodore 109

Kennington 73, 75
King's Arms, Sandford 77, 81
Kitchin, George W. 79, 111

Langford, Martha (later Prickett) 102
Lawrence, A. W. & T. E. 106
Liddell, Frederica 50
Liddell, Henry (1788–1872) 89, 93
Liddell, Rhoda xiii, 36, 89, 93
London Livery Companies
    Goldsmiths 117

Merchant Taylors 117
Skinners 118
Stationers 117, 118
Louse Lock, Oxford 32
Lutwidge, Lucy 30, 80

Macmillan, Alexander 31, 33
Mallinson, Arnold 26, 104
Martin, Robert Bernard 32
Masterman, J. C. 105, 106
Medley 15, 17, 20, 63, 118
Menzies, Fletcher 119
Millais, John 35
Millin, John & Mary 41
Mitre Inn, Oxford 103
Morrell's Brewery 67
Morris, Jan 25, 53
Morris, William (Lord Nuffield) 75,
    109
Morrish, Sir James 114
Museum of Oxford 118

Needham, Francis Charles 93
Newry, Lord 89, 93
Nuneham 10, 11, 18, 45, 79, 80, 87-97

Osney 9, 29, 30, 32, 35, 41, 46, 63, 101
Oxford Canal 32, 35, 82, 106
Oxford Castle 48
Oxford Colleges
    Balliol 66, 118
    Brasenose 118
    Corpus Christi 118
    Exeter 55, 117, 118
    Jesus 106, 118
    Keble 118
    Magdalen 52, 62, 106, 118
    New 110, 118
    Oriel 117, 120
    Pembroke 118
    Queen's 118
    St John's 118
    Trinity 64–66, 79, 103, 111, 118
    University 117
    Worcester 60, 78, 111

Oxford Movement 33
Oxford Parishes
  Holywell 82
  St Aldate's 103, 109
  St Clement's 102
  St Ebbe's 9
  St Michael at the Northgate 102
  St Peter-in-the-East 109
  St Thomas' 35
Oxford Streets
  Beaumont Street 102
  Cornmarket 110
  Cowley Road 102
  High Street 61, 103, 108–111, 113
  St Aldate's 41, 44, 106, 115, 118
Oxford University Boat Club 55, 57, 64,
  65, 112, 118, 121
Oxford University Press 30–35

'Pactolus' 47, 48, 121
Port Meadow 15–20, 23, 32, 63, 93, 100
Pre-Raphaelite Brotherhood 29, 30, 35,
  40, 93
Prickett, Althea 101, 104
Prickett family of Binsey 24, 25, 100-102,
  104
Prickett family of Thame 102
Prickett, Elizabeth (1837–1914) 103
Prickett, Frederick 103
Prickett, James & Elizabeth 25, 39, 48,
  102–104
Prickett, Mary 24, 25, 30, 39, 51–53, 61, 74,
  88, 89, 94, 95, 100, 102–104, 113
Prince & Princess of Wales (Edward
  VII) 36, 60, 61, 63–66, 71
Prince Leopold 71
Prout, Rev. Thomas Jones 22–26, 100
Pycroft, James 111, 120, 121

Radcliffe Observatory 10, 35
Radley 18
Randall, Elizabeth (later Stainer) 113, 114
Randall, Josiah 110
Randall, Thomas 54, 110–116, 121
Ranken, Rev. William Henry 79

Reeve (née Farr), Mrs Lorina 60
Rimmer, Alfred 3, 77
Rose Island 73–75
Rosebury, Lord 103
Rossetti, Dante Gabriel 35
Rugby school 57
Rundt, Carl 35
Ruskin, John 29, 35, 36, 53

St Barnabas', Jericho 31, 35
St Frideswide 23, 25, 26, 29, 36, 101–102
St Margaret's, Binsey 23, 25, 26, 101–102
St Paul's, Jericho xiv, 31, 35
Salter Brothers 37–39, 64, 96, 115, 118
Sandford-on-Thames 71, 77–82, 91, 118, 120
Savage, Robert 109
Seacourt 101
Sheepwash Channel 32
Shrimpton, T. & G. 67
Southey, Reginald 50, 58, 68
Spiers, Samuel Patey 103
Spiers, Richard James 103, 113, 115
Stainer, John & family 113

Taunt, Henry 1, 2, 20, 28, 54, 59, 73, 76, 86
Taunton, Elias 112
Tenniel, Sir John 12, 16, 31, 33, 40, 41, 81,
  83, 104–108, 115
Thame 25, 75, 100–102
'Thornbury' 25
Torpid races 56, 58, 60, 63, 66, 69
Tractarianism 33, 35
Trill Mill Stream 15, 39, 47, 48, 53, 105, 106,
  112, 121
Tuckwell, William 112, 119–121
Tumbling Bay 32

Whitburn (S. Tyne) 50
White stone days 4, 50, 61, 74, 75, 89, 90,
  94, 95
Wilde, Oscar 53
Wilson, Sir Angus 116
Wolvercote 109
Woolner, Thomas 31
Wytham 6, 18

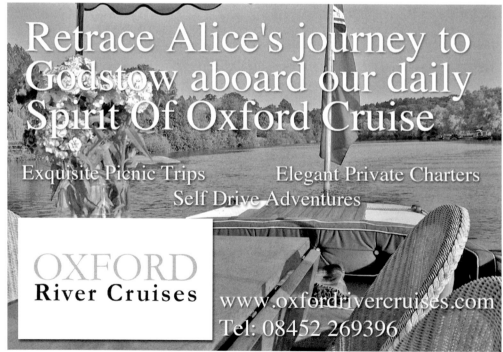

A Towpath Walk in Oxford

The Canal and River Thames between Wolvercote and the City

MARK DAVIES AND CATHERINE ROBINSON

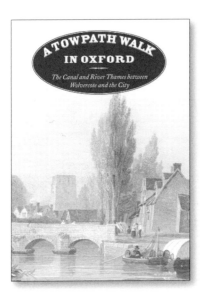

A *Towpath Walk in Oxford* takes the reader on a near-circular seven-mile route along the towpaths of central and north Oxford. Drawing on archive records and oral histories, *A Towpath Walk in Oxford* describes notable events and landmarks, and tells the stories of the characters – resourceful, eccentric, or notorious – who have shaped the varied waterway scene that Oxford enjoys today.

Includes detailed sections on Godstow, Port Meadow, Binsey, Medley, and Jericho.

"A remarkable compendium of historical fact and fiction concerning Oxford's waterways. It is equally readable as a practical walk guide or as a history book."
Canal Boat & Inland Waterways magazine

"At times like a pilgrimage, at times like a historical pub crawl
… the perfect combination."
Oxford Times Limited Edition magazine

"A most informative text which never loses sight of the human element
… a very easy read despite being choc-full with facts and details."
Canal & Riverboat magazine

"The whole book reads superbly." – *William Horwood, Oxford author*

"Beautifully done, a model of its kind." – *Margaret Drabble, novelist and critic*

Oxford Towpath Press ISBN 0 9535593 1 9
www.oxfordwaterwalks.co.uk

The Abingdon Waterturnpike Murder
A True-life Tale of Crime and Punishment

MARK DAVIES

The Abingdon Waterturnpike Murder investigates the brutal death of an elderly man on the edge of the Harcourt family home of Nuneham Park as he walked home from Abingdon's Michaelmas Fair in 1787. As events unfold, a wide-ranging, well-organised criminal underworld is revealed, and four local men are eventually held responsible. In the course of a story which ranges across Oxfordshire and Berkshire, and as far as London, many extraordinary, emotive, and shocking aspects of eighteenth-century life are revealed, along with the likelihood of a deliberate miscarriage of justice.

"Very readable and entertaining ... I enjoyed it immensely."
John Pilling, Principal Librarian, Oxfordshire County Council

"Wonderfully written and presented."
William Horwood, Oxford author

"As a snapshot of the seamier side of Abingdon life in the late eighteenth century this is a first-rate book."
St Michael's Parish magazine, Abingdon

"Reveals a world both distantly removed in time, but as hauntingly familiar as last week."
Canal and Riverboat magazine

"Fascinating, well-researched, written in a lively engaging style ... altogether admirable."
Dr John Curtis, Oxford historian

Oxford Towpath Press ISBN 0 9535593 2 7
www.oxfordwaterwalks.co.uk